PRAISE FOR *MANAGING MULTIPLE PROJECTS*

Elizabeth has presented at several eve... ... our Assistant community and written fantastic articles for our website. She is an expert in project management and always provides clear guidance and excellent strategies to those who need help managing multiple projects. I highly recommend her book and encourage anyone who has to manage projects to seek out her work.
Nicky Christmas, Founder and Editor of Practically Perfect PA

In this increasingly projectized world of portfolios, programs, multiple projects, tasks, contracts and virtual teams, in an ever more complex and uncertain environment, the challenges and stressors facing project professionals can be daunting. Elizabeth has taken on these challenges with knowledgeable, practical and very readable advice. She's one of the most creative project management experts that I know of. If you are working on two or more projects and want to be more successful and reduce stress, this book is for you.
David L Pells, Editor, *PM World Journal*

This practical and well-written guide uses a simple framework to help you manage your workload, combine project schedules and engage stakeholders across multiple projects. It also helps you optimize your personal productivity. Reading this book will increase the quality of your work and save you time in the long run.
Susanne Madsen, executive coach and author of *The Power of Project Leadership*

Elizabeth Harrin has written an excellent guidebook for project managers and others juggling multiple projects. Filled with practical advice on managing it all, you will become a better project manager. She lays out a framework that is easy to follow and will help you get control of your workload. To get the most out of this book, implement the action steps at the end of each chapter and check out the appendices to find helpful checklists and templates. I highly recommend this book.

Cornelius Fichtner, PMP, CSM, President of OSP International LLC, Founder of The Project Management PrepCast and Host of *The Project Management Podcast*

We are living in a time of mass disruption, and Elizabeth counsels us that so much can be solved with better planning and by being better organized. When so much feels outside of our control, Elizabeth brings us order by presenting various tools and techniques to help us create our own ways of working across waterfall, hybrid and agile approaches. Want to be a better project manager? Read this book, get a hold of these practices, and put them into action.

Brantlee Underhill, Managing Director, North America, Project Management Institute (PMI)

'Employee engagement has a direct correlation to productivity' and the importance of engaging with people, especially when working across multiple projects with varying deadlines and dependencies, has been documented perfectly in this book. As a professional managing multiple projects in my career this was a refreshing read, breaking down the plan concept across five main areas. Elizabeth's focus on the importance of people, engagement and communication was a pleasure to read, and a must for every project manager out there.

Nicola Graham, Managing Director, Simplify Change

Managing a project is tough – managing multiple projects can be overwhelming. To succeed, you need the skills of a juggler, a mind that can multi-process, and a spirit of adventure. A great reference guide can only be a bonus and this is exactly what you have in Elizabeth Harrin's book *Managing Multiple Projects* – a perfect partner to multiple project success.

Peter Taylor, author of *The Lazy Project Manager*

The reason lots of project people are down-trodden, overworked, underpaid and undervalued is because they appear as a level of effort line on the project plan. They're there, but no one knows what they really do – a non-value adding overhead. Elizabeth's book helps you become a benefits-driven portfolio. Rather than project managing others or blindly delivering tasks, it shows you how to better understand and manage yourself, but in a project and portfolio way. A strategic and self-reflective way. Poacher turned gamekeeper. The world needs smart citizens for the smart cities it needs to live in. This book will help you and help others make the world the better place it urgently needs to become.

Steve Wake, Chair, BSi MS/2, past APM Chair, Freeman of the Guild of Educators

In a world where everyone is increasingly expected to juggle multiple tasks, priorities and projects, this book is an important and much-needed resource. Combining useful insights from effective managers with meaningful reflection, it offers a practical and tailorable coaching manual designed to guide and support managers throughout their multi-project careers.

Professor Darren Dalcher, Director, National Centre for Project Management, Lancaster University Management School

Managing multiple projects is often neglected in project management theory and texts. So, it's about time we finally get a practical, no-nonsense guide that helps us deliver all our projects with their varying needs and stakeholders without burning out. Elizabeth knows her stuff!

Anita Phagura, Founder, Fierce Project Management

Organizations around the world are all suddenly demanding one key skill – the ability to manage multiple projects (MMP). The problem is that few people actually have this skill. This book shows how to rise to the challenge of MMP, make a fantastic contribution to your organization and still have a life. If you are facing MMP overload, this book should be No 1 on your infinite 'to-do' list. Read it now!

Stephen Carver, consultant, speaker and Senior Lecturer in Change and Crisis Management at Cranfield University School of Management

In work, there's no such thing as problems, merely the opportunity for projects and productivity. Elizabeth Harrin has written a thoughtful, detailed and useful guide to project management for smart people. It's packed with models, practical perspectives and some of the best thinking on being productive with the bigger picture. Whether your projects look like sushi, spaghetti or a side dish, this book will help you make sense of them and get your world under control.

Graham Allcott, Founder of Think Productive and author of *How to be a Productivity Ninja*

Managing Multiple Projects

*How project managers can balance priorities,
manage expectations and increase productivity*

Elizabeth Harrin

KoganPage

First published in Great Britain and the United States in 2022 by Kogan Page Limited

2nd Floor, 45 Gee Street
London
EC1V 3RS
United Kingdom
www.koganpage.com

8 W 38th Street, Suite 902
New York, NY 10018
USA

4737/23 Ansari Road
Daryaganj
New Delhi 110002
India

Kogan Page books are printed on paper from sustainable forests.

ISBNs
Hardback   978 1 3986 0552 7
Paperback 978 1 3986 0550 3
Ebook   978 1 3986 0551 0

British Library Cataloguing-in-Publication Data
A CIP record for this book is available from the British Library.

Library of Congress Cataloging-in-Publication Data
Names: Harrin, Elizabeth, author.
Title: Managing multiple projects: how project managers can balance priorities, manage expectations and increase productivity / Elizabeth Harrin.
Description: 1st Edition. | New York, NY: Kogan Page Inc, [2022] | Includes bibliographical references and index.
Identifiers: LCCN 2022005014 (print) | LCCN 2022005015 (ebook) | ISBN 9781398605527 (hardback) | ISBN 9781398605503 (paperback) | ISBN 9781398605510 (ebook)
Subject: Project Management
Classification: LCC HD69.P75 H35937 2022 (print) | LCC HD69.P75 (ebook) | DDC 658.4/04–dc23/eng/20220202
LC record available at https://lccn.loc.gov/2022005014
LC ebook record available at https://lccn.loc.gov/2022005015

Typeset by Hong Kong FIVE Workshop
Print production managed by Jellyfish
Printed and bound by CPI Group (UK) Ltd, Croydon CR0 4YY

CONTENTS

LIST OF FIGURES AND TABLES

TABLES

ABOUT THE AUTHOR

Elizabeth Harrin, MA, FAPM, MBCS has been actively engaged in projects since 2000. She works with individuals and organizations to help them deliver projects with more confidence and less stress.

Elizabeth gained her experience of leading complex projects through a career that spans financial services and healthcare, in the UK and France. She has managed teams leading a range of large- and small-scale projects from an Enterprise Resource Planning (ERP) implementation to compliance initiatives and IT-enabled business change. She has had to learn strategies to manage multiple projects throughout her work, both in her corporate roles at AXA and Spire Healthcare, and in her own business, Otobos Consultants Ltd, which provides corporate project management materials and support for individual project managers through training and mentoring.

She is the author of a number of other books about project management: *Shortcuts to Success: Project Management in the Real World* (BCS Books, 2013, which was a finalist in the Management Book of the Year Awards 2014 and now in its second edition), the PMI bestseller *Collaboration Tools for Project Managers* (PMI, 2016), *Communicating Change* (Bookboon, 2017), *Project Manager* (BCS, 2018), *Customer-Centric Project Management* (Gower, 2012) and *Engaging Stakeholders on Projects: How to Harness People Power* (APM, 2020). She has contributed chapters to several books and is widely published in magazines and websites on project management topics. Elizabeth is also the award-winning blogger behind A Rebel's Guide to Project Management, which aims to help teams get work done.

Elizabeth is a Fellow of the Association for Project Management and a member of the Project Management Institute (PMI). She holds degrees from the University of York and Roehampton University.

You can contact Elizabeth with feedback, questions or to find out about the group mentoring programme, Project Management Rebels. She also provides individual mentoring services.

LinkedIn: www.linkedin.com/in/elizabethharrin

Facebook community: www.facebook.com/groups/projectmanagementcafe

Speaking: www.elizabeth-harrin.com

Web: www.projectmanagementrebels.com

FOREWORD

Projects change the world. Projects make impossible dreams possible.

The behavioural and social sciences endorse the idea that there are a few ways of working and collaborating that are particularly motivating and inspiring for people working on a project. These are that a project should have ambitious goals, a higher purpose and a clear deadline. You have probably noticed that what people tend to remember most clearly from their entire careers is the projects they work on – often the successful ones, but also the failed ones.

According to recent research, the number of individuals working in project-based roles will increase from 66 million (in 2017) to 88 million (forecast 2027). And the value of economic activity worldwide that is project orientated will grow from $12 trillion (in 2013) to $20 trillion (forecast 2027).[1] Those are millions of projects requiring millions of project managers per year.

This is what I describe as the Project Economy, a term I conceived in 2018 when working on my earlier book, *The Project Revolution, How to Succeed in a Project Driven World.*

This silent disruption is impacting not only organizations but also the very nature of work, and our entire professional lives. The traditional one-company career path of previous generations is now a distant memory. Today, people happily and fruitfully change jobs and employers a number of times during their careers. I believe that this trend will accelerate and that professional careers will become a sequence of projects. Another notable trend related to this is the growth in self-employment – according to Quartz at Work, an HR consulting company, the number of Americans working for themselves could triple by 2020.[2] They will be, effectively, managing a portfolio of projects.

A global revolution

The more you look, the more projects you will see. On my desk, I have a bushel of examples.

For example, in December 2016, the US Senate unanimously approved the Program Management Improvement and Accountability Act (PMIAA),[3] which will enhance accountability and best practices in project and programme management throughout the US federal government. The PMIAA will reform federal programme management policy in four important ways: creating a formal job series and career path for programme and project managers in the federal government; developing a standards-based programme and project management policy across the federal government; recognizing the essential role of executive sponsorship and engagement by designating a senior executive in federal agencies to be responsible for programme and project management policy; and strategy sharing knowledge of successful approaches to programme and project management through an interagency council on programme and project management.

In the UK, on 6 January 2017, the Association for Project Management was awarded a Royal Charter.[4] The receipt of a Royal Charter marks a significant achievement in the evolution of project management and will have positive implications for those who make, and seek to make, a career in this field. The Charter recognizes the project management profession, rewards the association that champions its cause and provides opportunities for those who practise its disciplines.

The Richards Group is the largest independently owned ad agency in the US, with billings of $1.28 billion, revenue of $170 million and more than 650 employees. Stan Richards, its founder and CEO, removed almost all of its management layers and job titles, leaving only that of project manager.[5]

In another example, in 2016, Nike was looking to fill a vacancy at its European headquarters. The job description was Corporate Strategy & Development Manager for the European, Middle East and Africa (EMEA) Region. Such a job would traditionally entail strategic planning, market analysis and competitive intelligence competencies. To my surprise, instead the job was described as 'project management'. This meant that Nike was looking for someone who could implement transversal and strategic projects for its strategy function. This was a clear shift of focus and culture: from planning and day-to-day activities to implementation and projects. And Nike is not alone – I have seen similar job descriptions for strategy functions at UPS, Amazon and others.

In the project economy we are all project managers

For centuries, learning was achieved by memorizing hefty books and mountains of written material. Today, the leading educational systems, starting from early ages, apply the concept of teaching projects. Applying theories and experimenting through projects has proven to be a much better learning method, and soon it will become the norm.

Not so long ago, professional careers were made in only one organization. Throughout the 20th century, most people worked for a single company. Today, we are likely to work for several companies, and at some point we will most probably become self-employed, working primarily on projects. This sort of career is best approached as a set of projects in which we apply the lessons we have learned from previous jobs, companies and industries while developing ourselves for our next career move, often not known in advance.

The emergence of projects as the economic engine of our times is silent but incredibly disruptive and powerful. And this massive disruption is not only impacting the way organizations are managed. Every aspect of our lives is becoming a set of projects also.

Juggling multiple projects has become one of our major challenges, both as individuals as well as organizations, in our private and in our professional lives. Elizabeth Harrin's book on managing multiple projects is a timely resource – full of practical tools and real examples that will help you build the knowledge and skills to thrive in a project-driven world.

There are fewer 'low-cost' ways of working more inclusive, impactful, motivating and inspiring than being part of a project with an ambitious goal, a higher purpose, and a clear fixed deadline.

Antonio Nieto-Rodriguez

ABOUT ANTONIO NIETO-RODRIGUEZ

World Champion in Project Management | Thinkers50 & Top 30 Global Gurus | PMI Fellow & Past Chair | Professor | HBR Author | Founder Strategy Implementation Institute | Founder Projects & Co | Director PMO | Marshall Goldsmith Executive Coach

Author of the *Harvard Business Review Project Management Handbook* and four other books, Antonio is the creator of concepts such as the Project Economy and the Project Manifesto. His research and global impact in modern management have been recognized by Thinkers50. Former Chairman of the Project Management Institute, he is the founder of Projects & Co and co-founder of the Strategy Implementation Institute. He is a member of Marshall Goldsmith 100 coaches. You can follow Antonio through his LinkedIn Newsletter – Lead Projects Successfully – and website.

Notes

1 Project Management Job Growth and Talent Gap Report 2017–2027 (Project Management Institute, 2017), accessed 1 October 2018, https://www.pmi.org/-/media/pmi/documents/public/pdf/learning/job-growth-report.pdf?sc_lang_temp=en (archived at https://perma.cc/X3H6-HSSD).

2 "The Number of Americans Working for Themselves could Triple by 2020" (Quartz at Work), last modified 21 February 2018, https://work.qz.com/1211533/the-number-of-americans-working-for-themselves-could-triple-by-2020 (archived at https://perma.cc/2DQ3-4LJY).

3 "US Senate Unanimously Approves the Program Management Improvement and Accountability Act" (Project Management Institute), last modified 1 December 2016, https://www.pmi.org/about/press-media/press-releases/senate-program-management-act (archived at https://perma.cc/CJ7W-ECGX).

4 "APM Receives Its Royal Charter" (Association for Project Management), last modified 6 January 2017, https://www.apm.org.uk/news/apm-receives-its-royal-charter (archived at https://perma.cc/A42W-ST56).

5 "Stan Richards's Unique Management Style" (Inc.), accessed 1 October 2018, https://www.inc.com/magazine/201111/stan-richards-unique-management-style.html (archived at https://perma.cc/6ND8-267M).

PREFACE

In my corporate career, I went from managing one big project to managing several small (but, according to my sponsors, equally important) projects as a result of returning to work part-time after maternity leave. I had to quickly learn skills to juggle competing priorities and manage expectations from board level down. It required a whole new way of thinking about my workload and engaging with the people around me to keep everything moving forward – because even after I had prioritized my work, I was still expected to show some kind of progress on all my projects, even the ones at the bottom of the list.

I know I'm not alone. My research for this book has shown that more people manage multiple projects than single projects. Yet, if you read project management books or attend a course, you'll learn about the end-to-end approaches for managing a single piece of work. That's good. We need that. But we also need a practical approach for layering project upon project. That's what I wanted to do with this book. I wrote it for project managers, programme managers, executive assistants, researchers, change managers, product owners, account managers, team leaders, small business owners: people who have to juggle so many different initiatives that sometimes the workload feels overwhelming and you end up working evenings and weekends just to stay afloat.

There is no magic wand to being able to manage multiple projects, objectives and deadlines. First, you need solid project management skills so you can do the job of a project manager with ease. In other words, you understand the basics of project management and can apply them efficiently. You don't want to have to keep looking up how to create a Gantt chart or wondering what process or form to use for the next part of your work. Being comfortable with the basics of managing a project is a pre-requisite. This book won't teach you how to do that. We will not cover the process for managing one project, but there are many other great books that do. Instead, this book will show you that repeating the 'one project' method over and over for each project is inefficient. There is a better way, and you're about to learn it.

In 2020, I surveyed 220 project managers about the work they do and how they feel about it. I was surprised by the results. Only 15 per cent of people reported managing just one project. Everyone else in a project delivery role is juggling the priorities, expectations and responsibilities of more than one project simultaneously.

I suppose I should not have been that surprised. In 2019, I ran a six-month training and mentoring programme for project managers leading multiple projects that attracted 50 students from around the world. In 2021, I launched an online Mastering Multiple Projects course which had a first cohort of 81 students, and people continue to join. This book has been formed from my interest in this topic over the past few years, and is deepened by my understanding of the real-life situations in which project managers find themselves.

Those situations are often hard. Project managers – in my experience – tend to be people passionate about doing a good job, and they hold themselves to high standards. Combine that with an increased workload and it's a helter-skelter ride to self-doubt and burnout.

That is perhaps part of the issue around why about 35 per cent of experienced project managers from my research say that they are considering leaving project management: the burden is too much. That alone has a massive implication for the future of project success. PMI reports that by 2027 the demand for project-orientated jobs is due to grow by 33 per cent (22 million jobs – see https://www.pmi. org/learning/careers/job-growth (archived at https://perma.cc/3Z2V-3EX2)). If the profession is losing experienced project managers because of what the job has become, then what does that mean for the projects planned for the future?

I feel it's crucially important that we equip today's and tomorrow's project managers (and people doing the role with a different title) with a realistic expectation of what it means to do the job – and the skills to manage multiple projects at the same time.

This book can't fix all the reasons people might choose to leave a project management job. What it can do is share with you my proven techniques, blending formal project management practices with time management and productivity tools in a framework to help you get out of overwhelm and fall back in love with managing projects. I hope this book begins a conversation about what the workload of a project manager is really like, and how, as a profession, we can shape the tools and processes we use to serve us better.

Elizabeth, West Sussex, 2021

Supporting resources for this book can be found at **koganpage.com/managing-multiple-projects** and **elizabeth-harrin.com/mmp**.

ACKNOWLEDGEMENTS

I'd like to thank Penny Pullan for helping me take the first steps with making this book into a reality, and for inspiring me to turn Chapter 1 into a quick start guide for this book.

I would also like to thank Isabelle Cheng, Amy Minshall, Adam Cox, Ryan Norman and the rest of the team at Kogan Page for seeing the potential in this book. Gillian Hutchison did a great job of helping me pull it all together and Ian B created the fantastic graphics.

Many people have kindly shared their unique insights into the world of work as they see it, and helped me stretch my understanding of the challenges faced in a diverse society. Special thanks are due to Anita Phagura, who listened without judgement, Hannah Bullard and Rebecca Alley, and Brian King for his input on neurodiversity (and Matthew Fox for putting us in touch).

I'm grateful to all of those who completed my survey about what it's like to manage multiple projects. Many of their stories are included throughout this book including Kelly, Omar, Juan Manuel, Robert V, Kirsten, David, Lisa, Dana, Leah, Erac, Dorte, Megan, Rachel, Stephene, Steph, Abigail, Else, Jen, Una, Amanda, Ana, Chet, Kelly, Akola, Alyssa, Sheri and Kimberly. Others contributed anonymously and I'm indebted to so many for sharing their experiences. Thank you!

My thanks also go to my past and present students and mentees, especially those in my virtual mentoring group, Project Management Rebels, who have taught me so much about the challenges of managing projects and continue to reinforce my belief that static textbook approaches rarely solve our problems in the real world.

I also want to acknowledge the limitations of my knowledge of the experience of neurodiverse project managers and team members, and the experience of people of colour and those with disabilities working in a project environment. I'm aware that my privilege shapes my interactions with stakeholders and decision-makers, as well as how I choose to spend my time. I've tried to include diverse voices, and to reflect the community of students and mentees I have worked with over the years.

My family continues to support me in creating time to work on book projects; picking up my share of the load while my head is somewhere in research or writing. Thanks are always due to Jon, Jack and Oliver, and my parents.

Introduction

Your manager might not say it, but more projects are coming your way. It might not be written in your role profile, but your boss expects you to juggle several things at once.

Project management is changing: as more and more work is done in a project-led way, teams are using tried-and-tested tools for smaller initiatives as well as those multi-million organizational transformation projects. And those smaller projects often can't justify the need for a full-time team.

Today, many people's work environment includes more knowledge work. There are more change initiatives to contribute to and get done. You're expected to have the skills to cope with a greater workload. Efficiency, project management tools and streamlined processes help teams deliver more with less time, and to manage the mental overhead of keeping many strands of work on the go at the same time.

At least, that's the expectation. However, most people have never been taught how to juggle multiple projects. Books (including the ones I have written) and training courses focus on the skills required to run one project, not how to combine and consolidate, merging plans and meetings, to deal with more than one at a time. So we muddle through, often inefficiently, using what we have been taught and hoping for the best.

The trouble with that approach is that when the systems for multi-project management aren't in place, you can feel overwhelmed with it all. And it's not as easy as simply overlaying the project process several times because that adds time and bulk to your work without necessarily adding anything of value. Managing multiple projects with competing deadlines can take it out of you. Here's the truth: without the skills to manage multiple projects, you'll crash and burn. It is no surprise that workload is the top cause of burnout (Moss, 2021). I've seen burnout happen to colleagues, and I've been on the verge of it myself (fortunately I managed to change my situation before it became crippling).

When I first started getting more and more projects added to my workload, I faced two choices: do the extra work and work more hours, or don't do it and take the career implications of being seen to not deliver. Neither of those are great choices, to be honest. Instead, I decided to rethink the way I handled my workload. I got good at the fundamental skills of being able to manage a multi-project environment by working on the following:

- Managing my own time: becoming personally good at time management and working efficiently.

- Managing work requests from others: I doubled-down on stakeholder engagement and building good relationships so I could push back politely but effectively when I needed to.

- Managing communication: I made sure everyone knew what was expected of them, what was going on and when deadlines were coming up so teams avoided rework, duplication of effort and I wasn't bothered with requests for status updates outside of the established communication schedules.

- Managing schedules: I became a power user for my software tools, so I could rely on them, and invested time in detailed planning to work out when stuff needed to happen so nothing fell through the cracks.

- Managing my environment: I systemized and checklist-ized as much as I could to have standard operating procedures for streamlining the work, thus reducing the amount of information I needed to actively hold in my brain.

You can do the same. When you are leading several initiatives simultaneously, you need to apply the skills you already have in different ways to maximize your time. Having the skills, tricks, processes, experience, knowledge – whatever you want to call it, and it's a blend of all of those – to keep multiple projects happening, moving forward, being seen to deliver AND get home on time… that's the secret to being able to meet your manager's expectations and avoid the burnout.

Protecting your mental and physical health (and that of your team) should be one of your key priorities. It was something I didn't realize until much further along in my project management career. I figured I would always be able to do it all, but actually I couldn't. For me, it was balancing work with being the kind of parent I wanted to be. Whether you want time to go to the gym on a work day, or have time to spend with your family, or time to unwind with the TV and a glass of wine at the end of the day (instead of doing emails until 11pm and then rolling exhausted into bed), you need to make that happen because no one else will actively manage it for you.

Juggling multiple projects is a challenge and a skill. And when you get it right it's rewarding. You get to meet more people, deliver more value and have variety in the day to keep your job interesting. But it does come with the risk of overwhelm, which is why going home on time should definitely be on your 'must do' list. I know: it's not always possible as a project manager to make it out of the office on time every day. In fact, the more senior I got in my corporate job, the more likely it was that there was some kind of issue to handle that couldn't wait until the next day. However, you should get to leave on time at least some of the time. The more you can manage your own diary, prioritize your workload and make progress during the normal working day, the easier it is to manage your time to at least get away from your desk at a reasonable time, some of the days.

This book will help you achieve that. You've picked up this book because you're prepared to learn something new about managing your workload, and you're in the right place. *Managing Multiple Projects* is a book to help you develop the skills and knowledge for juggling multiple projects, dealing with conflicting priorities and managing expectations… and still leave the office on time. It aims to improve the chances of project success by giving you the tools you need to get everything done without burning out.

Whether you work in an informal project management role, on a couple of large projects or multiple smaller projects, you face the challenge of keeping all the information straight in your head and meeting the requirements of multiple bosses. This book will help you address those challenges and give you tips and techniques to streamline what's filling up your To Do list. You won't need to get permission for a whole new way of working either: these are changes you can make for yourself to win back more time in your day.

Managing Multiple Projects takes you on a step-by-step journey to critically review your workload and make changes in how you work to be more efficient. You'll learn a framework based on five concepts to help tame the chaos of multiple projects, leading to (hopefully) more confidence that you are making the right kind of progress.

The managing multiple projects framework

FIGURE 0.1   The managing multiple projects framework

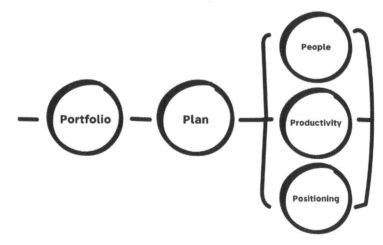

Figure 0.1 shows the managing multiple projects framework. It's not truly linear because not much in project management is. Most methods for getting work done require review and reflection so the

'step-by-step to a specific end goal' is rarely the perfect answer to the complexities of the modern work environment. There are too many complications and diversions that get in the way!

Instead, think of the framework as the five concepts that will help you feel more in control of your workload. It does help to have an understanding of your personal work portfolio before you try to plan your activities for the next few months, but if you want to dive into personal productivity first, for example, skip ahead to Chapter 6. The pieces of the framework are:

Portfolio: This is where you gain a consolidated understanding of your current workload in a way that helps you see patterns and groupings across all the things you are doing. You will be equipped to talk about your workload in a different way – using portfolio management principles – and get tools to prioritize what you have to do.

Plan: This is where you combine your project schedules to give you a holistic, big picture overview plan of all your responsibilities. You will learn to look at task scheduling in different ways to help you make better decisions about where to spend your time and to avoid wasting effort on planning work that will have changed by the time you get to it. This overview will inform whether you can take on additional work and when, by improving visibility of what you are already committed to in the coming weeks and months.

People: This part of the framework teaches you how to engage and work with the most influential stakeholders – the people who are interested in and impacted by your projects, and those who have to contribute to the work. You will learn how to keep track of all the people you work with and how to prioritize your time with them. Just as project schedules overlap, so too do people's interests. When you understand how your stakeholders interact with your various projects, you can use their time more efficiently too.

Productivity: The best processes in the world won't help if you feel personally disorganized and struggling with productivity. While productivity looks and feels different to different people, there are some common elements that many people find challenging. In this part of the framework, you will learn tips and tricks for managing your own work and creating focus time in your week to dedicate to the tasks that are a priority for you.

Positioning: Finally (although it doesn't have to come last in your learning), you will find it easier to be successful if your wider environment is set up for success. Many people managing projects are not the top leaders in their organizations and can't influence strategy, what tools are in use, or how many projects the business promises to clients. This section is about looking for things you can influence that will make your life easier and support your colleagues at the same time, such as by creating processes and checklists to make work repeatable and standardized. That takes away some of the mental overload of having to think of what to do all the time so you can use your brainpower for more value-added tasks instead.

The framework is designed to be scalable whether you are managing two projects or 22 (hopefully you aren't managing 222). You can take the pieces of it that feel the most important to you and use those, or adopt the whole thing as an extension to the way you work today. As you go through the book, make choices about how you can implement these tips, tools and tactics. If you go all in, use Appendix 3 as your implementation roadmap.

A book about project management is always a book about working with others and understanding the nuances of organizational culture. All workplaces are different, so while this book gives you a framework and techniques for managing multiple projects, feel free to adapt the ideas to make them fit better to where you work and how you work. Take what works, adapt what doesn't fit your working preferences and ignore what you know would be a disaster in your workplace – although perhaps test it out in a small way first, just to be sure!

How this book is organized

This book is organized into seven chapters. Chapter 1 is your quick start guide. Here you'll find fast answers to urgent questions. If you're struggling with something right now, flip to this section, find your problem and then be guided to the part of the book that will help you the most.

Chapter 2 discusses the realities of managing multiple projects. You'll learn why it isn't easy and what warning signs to look for. You'll discover a new way of thinking about your workload: do you have sushi, spaghetti or side dish projects?

Chapter 3 covers the first concept in the framework for busting the overwhelm and managing all your projects, which is the Portfolio. It gives you the tools to create your personal work portfolio. You'll get a better understanding of your workload and be able to prioritize efficiently – both your project work and everything else that fits around the edges of that.

Chapter 4 talks about how to combine project schedules to give you visibility of your upcoming deadlines across all your projects. Multi-project scheduling is a skill you will need to develop to make sure no work falls through the cracks. This chapter covers the second concept in the framework, Plan, and shows you how to manage dependencies and create fully integrated or high-level plans, as well as co-ordinating the work of the people allocated to do the tasks.

The third concept in the framework is People. Chapter 5 is your guide to engaging stakeholders across multiple projects. It covers the interpersonal skills required to manage incoming requests for work and to engage outwards as well: up, across and down the organization so that everyone knows what's happening on all your projects in a timely way. You'll learn how to prioritize between stakeholders, avoid communications fatigue in stakeholders, and to set and manage expectations effectively. This chapter also covers how to consolidate meetings and reports to save you time.

Chapter 6 is all about managing your own time, because the fourth concept in the framework is Productivity. We'll take a practical look at how to make the most of your working hours, ensuring you can make progress on all your projects. This chapter discusses three productivity saboteurs: things that stop you being productive and what you can do about them. It will also equip you to have a structured conversation with your manager if you really do have more work than any human could realistically be expected to do with the time available, because no productivity approach in the world can help you if that's the case.

Finally, Chapter 7 looks at the last concept in the framework, which is Positioning. You'll learn how to set yourself and your environment up for success. That section of the book talks about ways to tweak your processes and influence those in use in your team so that they are more standardized, repeatable and easier to follow. It also covers governance in a multi-project environment and the minimal amount of documentation you can (normally) get away with to save you time.

You will find action steps and key takeaways at the end of most chapters. Think of these as your homework assignments: it's a good first step to read a book, but you won't actually see any improvement in how you manage multiple projects unless you take some action to do things differently. You don't have to do the action steps during your first read. Go through the book to familiarize yourself with the framework, the ideas and concepts, and then read it again with a view to taking action towards creating your own multi-project management system. As we've seen, there are five concepts within the framework: Portfolio, Plan, People, Productivity and Positioning. You can work through them one at a time, perhaps taking a concept per week (or month) to implement in your own work.

I recommend you block out some time in your calendar now to reflect on your current working practices, use the templates and review the material. Take as much time as you need to have conversations with relevant colleagues and to get any support you need from your team and organization to put the ideas in this book into practice.

Finally, you will find Appendices at the end of the book to help you take action. Appendix 1 has checklists that cover regular tasks that project managers do on a daily, monthly, weekly and annual basis. Use them as a prompt to ensure all of your projects are making progress and getting the attention they deserve, because it is easy to overlook the basics when work gets busy. They should act as a starting point for your own work checklists: as you'll see as you go through the book, the more activities you can put into templates and lists, the less information you have to hold in your head which alleviates some of the burden of juggling lots of projects. Appendix 2 gives you a simple weekly report template for sharing status updates on multiple projects at the same time. Appendix 3 is a guide to implement the framework and put into practice what you have learned from this book. To help reflect on your experiences and action-taking, Appendix 4 is a Stop, Start, Continue exercise that you can use alone or with your team.

Reference

Moss, J (2021) *The Burnout Epidemic: The rise of chronic stress and how we can fix it*, Harvard Business Review Press, Boston

01

Quick start guide: fast answers to urgent questions

Have you picked up this book wanting to solve a particular problem? This section will help! Let's get you unstuck with some fast answers to common questions. Find your challenge below for a quick answer and then flick to the relevant section of the book to take it further.

I've been asked to do another project and I don't know how to tell my manager I'm already drowning.

Your manager probably doesn't have the full picture about what you are doing. Turn to Chapter 3 and start putting together your personal portfolio so you can both see what's currently on your To Do list. Look at how many hours you are spending on each item per week and estimate what the latest project will take.

Next, arrange to meet your manager and ask the question, 'I'm already working at full capacity on the projects on this list. What do you want me to slow down or stop so I can focus on this? Can you help me with the prioritization of my workload so I'm working on the initiatives that are the most value, as we're now at the point where there is too much for me to deliver everything within the timescales we've already discussed?'

Hopefully that will prompt an open discussion about prioritizing the work. If slowing down or stopping certain activities is not an option, move to talking about who else could pick up some of the tasks. Shifting work around within the team is also a solution to one person being overloaded (as long as the person being delegated to has the time available).

What should I do first? I have so much on my To Do list and I don't know how to prioritize what's important.

First, breathe! A long list of projects always feels overwhelming. The goal is to understand what you are prioritizing and then prioritize the work. Chapter 3 has four options for prioritizing your work. Read those and have a go at using one (or more) of them to put your workload into an order that feels manageable.

Part of the challenge of managing multiple projects is that priorities often change. Set some time aside each week to review whether your list still represents what is actually a priority. Prioritization is not a one-and-done thing, so having that mindset will help you moving forward.

I'm spending too much time in the details and I don't really know where my work is going.

Turn to Chapter 4 which will help you take a big picture look at your work to spot patterns and groupings. Thinking differently about 'all the things' will help you see how tasks and projects fit together towards larger goals which should alleviate some of the concern that you don't know what your work is leading up to.

I'm spending so much time entering tasks into software and designing schedules for my work that I don't have enough time to actually do the tasks themselves. What should I be doing differently?

Let's go back to basics: why are you doing so much planning? What's the problem you are trying to solve with that? What are you trying to find out? The answer will help you determine what the best next steps will be. For example, if the goal is to identify pinch points for resources, that's a different challenge from trying to create timeline information for a status report, or to support a conversation you have scheduled with your manager about how busy you are.

It's OK to do a quick scribbled schedule on your notepad, or a summary view of the next six months in a spreadsheet, especially if it is not something you have to come back to or update.

If planning in detail is the problem, then turn to the section in Chapter 4 on rolling wave planning and see if that technique will give you enough detail to keep the work moving forward without being bogged down in tasks for the future.

I've just realized my calendar for next month is awful. I have loads of important deliverables due and I'm going to be exhausted. How can I stop this happening again?

When you manage each project independently, you can't easily see what the bigger picture impact will be on you or other people in your team. Chapter 4 will help you set up systems to consolidate your schedules and spot where your busy times will be so you can plan accordingly. Organizing child and elder care, meal planning and trying to get ahead on non-work tasks (like buying and writing all the birthday cards for the month in advance and leaving them by the door to post on the right days) can help. If you can, in the future try to organize work so there aren't too many big events in your projects happening at the same moment.

It feels like something is always falling through the cracks and I don't know how to stay on top of everything.

That's the reason I wrote this book! Too much of my corporate career was feeling like I was holding things together by a thread. And many of the project managers I mentor or chat to on social media say the same. Turn to Chapter 6 which will help you take a critical look at how you work. It has tips for personal time management and strategies for organizing your tasks to stay on top of everything.

Chapter 6 covers the Productivity concept of the framework that this book will help you implement to get on top of your work and be more efficient. Using those strategies, you will (hopefully) start feeling like you are on top of things because you will have full visibility of your work and techniques to streamline what you do. That's not to say you will end up with hours of extra time for sunbathing and cocktails on a Friday afternoon, but the goal is to give you practical solutions for taking back control.

I don't have enough time to talk to all my stakeholders.

That's normal! If you've got many projects on the go, the number of stakeholders you have increases. You'll be working with people across many teams and they will all have different expectations of you and the work you are doing.

While it would be lovely to think we could treat all stakeholders with equal attention and dedicate adequate time to each and every one, there aren't enough hours in the day. Instead, like with projects, we have to prioritize our engagements with people. Chapter 5 will give you the tools to do this, so you can invest more time with the stakeholders who have the biggest influence on your work.

Stakeholder influence and interest changes over time, so your 'priority' stakeholders may well shift as you go through the project. Make sure you are regularly reviewing who is getting the most of your attention so you can be confident it's going to the right people.

I'm in meetings all the time. I want to cut the number of meetings I'm having.

You are in full control of how many meetings you organize. If you are the meeting organizer, rethink what meetings you are in and whether they really need to be a meeting or not. For example, change weekly team meetings to fortnightly, if that would still give you the same (or a good enough) outcome. Change the duration of meetings to be 10 to 15 minutes less than what you currently have scheduled. Check out Chapter 5 for information on combining meetings so you don't need to have so many.

If you are being invited to meetings all the time, reconsider whether you actually need to be there. Could you delegate your attendance to someone else? Could you attend only for a portion of the meeting where points relevant to you will be discussed? Ask the organizer: 'I'll join the meeting for that agenda point. When do you need me to dial in/join?' Set the expectation that you will not be there for the whole thing.

There will always be meetings where you have to coach the team through to a decision or conclusion, and those are the ones you don't want to miss. However, the more you have confidence in your colleagues, the easier it is to let them have meetings without you. If you are only sitting in to make sure the meeting happens, or because they have asked you to organize it, then show up for the first ten minutes to set the scene and give them some direction, and then leave. If necessary, join again towards the end to listen to the team feed back the output and actions.

You will know if it's a meeting that is going to be useful and relevant or one that will suck the life out of you and deliver nothing of value. If it's the latter, take a big breath and hit decline on the invite. Perhaps add a note along these lines:

- 'I'm unable to attend, but I can send you a written update the day before to share with the group.'

- 'Based on the agenda, I don't think you need me this early/late in the discussion. Can you copy me in on the minutes instead? Thanks!'

- 'I didn't see an agenda for this meeting so I'm not sure if I can add any value to the topics being discussed. Is there anything specific you need from me at this time?'

- 'I see you already have Person A attending, so I think our area is adequately covered and as I have a clash at that time I'll let them fill me in afterwards.'

- 'Thanks for including me, but I don't think I'm the right person. Would you like me to check if Person B can attend instead?'

How do I manage my projects when my resources keep getting pulled on to other work? I don't have line management authority over the people, so I feel like I'm having to ask my colleagues for favours just to get business critical projects done.

Projects that are a priority for you are not always a priority for other people, especially if those colleagues have day jobs that are involved in handling company operations, like serving customers or, as we used to say in IT, 'keeping the lights on'. Day jobs take priority over project work, which is often treated as discretionary.

However, if your project is truly business critical, you need support from senior managers to make sure the team leaders of your resources understand that. A lot of project management is negotiating and influencing, so use those skills to have conversations with your manager and their managers, as well as project sponsors. Ideally, you would want ring-fenced, dedicated time from those resources so they can complete their project tasks. Look at the section on planning time with other people in Chapter 5 for ideas on how to build success-ful working relationships with these stakeholders – so you can be more influential when you need to be.

If that isn't possible, and you are still not receiving the support you require, work out what the impact of the delay will be. For example, it's not really about implementing a new process by the planned date. It's really about improving staff satisfaction in time for the annual survey, or getting the time-saving benefits of ten minutes per day per team member, which equates to efficiency savings the organization isn't getting for every week of delay.

Ultimately, it's easier to secure resources for your projects if every-one has the same idea about what is a company priority, so everyone's work objectives and targets are aligned behind common goals.

I'm constantly switching between projects. How do you manage all the multi-tasking?

I don't! Most of the time I time-block my day so I have fewer things to deal with at any one time. You can do the same. For exam-ple, where it is within your power to do so, only book meetings for certain days of the week. If someone asks you when you are available to meet, don't reply, 'Whenever'. Tell them the days that you accept meetings: 'Any Tuesday, Wednesday or Thursday works for me.'

Block out other periods of time for report writing, responding to emails, project work or something else. Remember that you don't have to answer every email within 30 seconds or pick up every call. If you know it's not urgent, let phone calls go to voicemail and call them back when you've finished your task. In most situations, people will have no issue with waiting an hour to talk to you.

Chapter 6 has more ideas for keeping focused on work: it's all about being intentional with how you spend your time while knowing that some curveball is likely to come and change your plans at the last minute.

I feel like I'm the only one having to juggle multiple projects and I'd like to hear about other people in the same situation.

You are definitely not alone! You'll find examples, anecdotes and stories of how other people deal with the challenges of managing multiple projects throughout the book. Perhaps some of their strategies and tips will help you think differently about your own workload.

Reading isn't enough for me. I want to be able to turn the strategies into action as I know I need to do things differently.

This book will give you five concepts within a framework for managing multiple projects. You'll find action steps at the end of each chapter. Work through those and you'll be on your way to using your new knowledge in a practical way. There is also a complete list of action steps in the form of an implementation plan in Appendix 3. Why not team up with a colleague to implement one part of the framework per month?

I don't think a particular tool, tip or technique will work for me (or someone on my team). What should I do?

You know your working style better than I ever could, and you also know your professional environment. There are no hard and fast rules in this book. Feel free to take what works and ignore what you know will not be successful in your environment. Tailor the ideas to fit ways of working that you feel comfortable with. Having said that, it might be worth giving the idea a go before you skip over it. How could you adapt it that would make it suitable for you?

I don't know what I want to know... but I want to learn as much as I can!

You're in the right place! Once you've read this book, take a look at the further reading and references as they will help you stretch your knowledge further. Remember, however, that learning is not the same as doing: while I've always found reading to be a valuable source of information and inspiration, you have to do something differently to get different results, so block out some time to work on the action steps and to consider how you can implement what you learn.

02

Why managing multiple projects is different

Around a third of the gross domestic product (GDP) in the average Western economy is a result of project activity (Schoper et al, 2018) so it is unsurprising that organizations do so many projects. They are the way strategy gets delivered, and in what the Project Management Institute (PMI) calls the 'project economy' (Anderson, 2019), it's likely that organizations will continue to deliver work through the structure of projects.

However, because there are so many projects, we all often have to contribute (or lead) several at a time. That makes multi-project management an expectation in many roles, so let's unpack that for a moment.

If you are managing multiple projects, it means you have more than one project on the go at the same time. You will have different project teams (even if the people on them are the same people). You might have different sponsors or customers, all with their own expectations of what is possible, and probably the belief that their project is the most important. Each project has its own timeline and you have to manage your time to keep them all moving forward to hit the planned deadlines and milestones. This workload is different from the workload of someone managing a single project, or carrying out their day job. There are more moving parts and normally more people involved.

In this chapter, you'll learn about what a multi-project environment is like, the different ways projects fit into your workload, and the warning signs to watch for that show you need to adapt the way you work before the risk of burnout becomes real.

Understanding the multi-project environment

Managing multiple projects is different from having responsibility for just leading one project. That's not to say that leading a single project is easy: the larger the project, the more complex and strategically important it tends to be, and that comes with its own stressors.

A multi-project environment features the following:

- A large number of unrelated stakeholders who need to be engaged in various, sometimes isolated, sometimes connected activities.

- More project sponsors to please.

- More expectations to meet.

- Project teams made up of part-time resources who also have a day job to do that takes priority over their project work.

- More resource conflicts to resolve, often with subject matter experts booked to work on multiple projects who then struggle to see their whole work commitments and aren't able to complete their tasks in the timeframe they expected.

- Constant pressure from deadlines instead of the comfortable ebb and flow of busy and not-so-busy points on a single project: every month one of your projects is beginning, completing or hitting a major milestone.

A workload that includes multiple projects also requires a slightly different take on the core skills that are used to manage a single project. It's not a totally new skillset, but it's a smarter, more complex way of addressing the work and the complexities of balancing many people, processes and products.

I started in project management working for an insurance firm as part of a team leading on the upgrade of a website. This project went smoothly with everyone knowing what they were supposed to do and hitting their deadlines. Later in my career, I progressed to working on a larger project to deliver a new IT system to 35 locations. While the size, scope and length of this project was greater than what I'd done before, similarities remained that helped me understand and manage the individual tasks.

However, at the next stage in my career, I was no longer leading groups of related projects and sometimes my stakeholders were totally different groups. I was team leader for a group of project managers, and I picked up some operational tasks, such as liaising with suppliers for ongoing contracts, that were nothing to do with my projects. When my sponsor informed me of another project coming my way it felt like the mental load of juggling so many things was going to be too much – even though I could make time for the physical workload.

During the experience I described above, my work was no longer a personal portfolio of connected and contextually relevant work – you will learn more about this in Chapter 3. Every day was a balance between doing something to advance my own To Do list and also supporting my team and colleagues with their work. What should I be focused on? How do I choose what to do first? How can I use what I already know to make this easier?

Those are some of the challenges of delivering multiple projects, and you'll learn more about the tools, tips and strategies for managing those challenges as you go through the book.

How projects fit into your job

Whether you have the job title of project manager or not, you could have a workload made up predominantly of projects. Perhaps the bulk of your time is spent in an operational role, with the expectation that you will manage projects around the edges of that.

Your project workload is likely to fit into one of three categories, depending on how it integrates into the rest of what you do. Let's look at those categories now.

Sushi

Just like a plate of perfect pieces of sushi, each of your projects are unrelated and stand well on their own. Project work is the main portion of your job and you have a number of initiatives on the go at any one time, varying in length of time, size and complexity. The projects are for various customers or sponsors and you have to work with a wide range of stakeholders, often influencing across different departments to secure the input and support you need.

Examples:

- Executive assistant leading various projects for many directors.
- Project manager in a small business supporting all the change projects the company wants to do.

Spaghetti

Like a tangle of spaghetti in a bowl, your workload is made up of several related projects. You do a wide variety of project work but it's broadly all thematically grouped and often the project teams are made up of the same people time after time. Your projects might affect a number of teams, but they all fall under the leadership of one director or under one team structure.

Examples:

- Project manager running a range of projects for one customer/ sponsor.
- Project manager setting up the same software or process for many customers.

Side dish

Projects are the 'side dish' to your day job. You have an operational role where projects are not your main focus, but you are still expected to manage small, short projects (and sometimes larger ones) around your other responsibilities. The content and customers for these projects can vary.

Examples:

- Team leader running a customer services department who also has to implement process improvements.
- Lawyer with a case load who also has to lead an internal change project to move the department to digital records.

> As a senior project management leader in a clinical team, all my projects fell under the umbrella of things that were to do with clinical operations, for example, projects that affected doctors, nurses, healthcare IT and so on. One of the things I did when I was in that role was also supporting hospital audits. Audits were an ongoing responsibility for the department and they were managed as small projects in their own right. My workload was a mix of strategic initiatives for executive sponsors and smaller projects: all related by the common themes of shared stakeholders and clinical work.

You may find that your project workload changes from time to time depending on what your organization requires of you. For example, a finance manager may find themselves spending more and more time on improvement projects during the majority of the year, and then be fully focused on year-end accounting when it's time to do the books for the past 12 months. A project manager with a spaghetti workload may be required to move to the sushi model when their manager changes suddenly and departmental priorities shift. Normally, project managers with spaghetti or sushi workloads also have business-as-usual or non-project tasks to do as well, and there's a list of common 'extras' in Chapter 3.

If you've only recently been given a couple of projects to manage, you might be feeling OK about your workload at the moment, whatever it looks like. The default approach most people use is to replicate the same methods as you use to run a single project. Just repeat exactly what you are doing for your first project, using the same approach, tools and techniques.

However, it won't be long before you start to feel that you don't have time to do everything to the level of quality you expect of yourself. You recognize that things aren't going as well as they could, and you feel it should be easier to work efficiently with a multi-project workload. That's the moment to check for the warning signs that tell you it's time to start doing things differently.

I had eight ongoing projects at one time. Some were third party software implementations and some were internal development. Some projects and teams were larger and required more time and effort (over a year duration) and some were small teams that were short term (three to four months) and less than five team members. The hardest part was keeping notes and communication with all the project team members – many overlapped on the projects.

One of the internal development projects included a large group of users. Testing was difficult and the team was over-critical at times, which slowed progress. Two projects were third party software that also included many of the same team members. I visited every project task list every day, made myself reminders on my calendar and tried to get communication/project updates out to the team quickly after meetings. I learned that there is no such thing as over-communicating, especially related to tasks due and planning for the next meeting. Next time I would try to organize tasks by team member across all projects to reduce the number of reminders/emails sent and to make it easier to check them off and track in PM software.

Kelly, PMP, PMI-ACP, senior project manager, USA

Key skills for managing projects

There are lots of reasons why projects don't always go to plan. In a study of more than 28 publications, researchers found 44 different 'failure factors' that influenced project outcomes for the worse (Rezvani and Khosravi, 2020). The top seven from that list – the things that come up time and time again in case studies and research papers – are:

1 Poor planning or unclear initial requirements;

2 Changing project requirements;

3 Poor communication and stakeholder relationships;

4 Lack of effective leadership;

5 Instability of the project team;

6 Poor risk management;

7 Poor project control.

If we flip those causes of failure into what it takes to be successful at leading projects, we get the following skills:

1 Planning;

2 Requirements management;

3 Communication and stakeholder engagement;

4 Leadership;

5 Team management;

6 Risk management;

7 Project control and governance.

Every project management professional has their own take on what the most important skills are for leading successful projects, but that's a pretty good list. However, when we adapt the list for what it looks like in a multi-project environment, we can see that the skills are the same but with a slightly different twist:

1 Planning (with an understanding of competing priorities between projects);

2 Requirements management (across projects that may be interconnected);

3 Communication and stakeholder engagement (with more people);

4 Leadership (in multiple leadership roles at a time on different initiatives);

5 Team management (with team members who might contribute to more than one team or project);

6 Risk management (where risks may aggregate across multiple projects to have a more significant impact);

7 Project control and governance (the time for which is squeezed in a multi-project environment because there are just so many other things to do).

Perhaps unsurprisingly, in a survey for this book (Harrin, 2021) planning and stakeholder engagement came out as the top skills required for people managing multiple projects, closely followed by team management (there's more on the resource management challenge in Chapter 4), as shown in Figure 2.1. In fact, survey respondents recognized over 60 different skills, from attention to detail to vendor management.

FIGURE 2.1   Top skills required for managing multiple projects

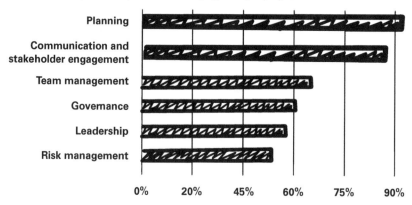

Warning signs to look out for in multi-project environments

If your working environment has some of the features discussed earlier in this chapter, then you are probably already spending at least some of your time feeling overwhelmed. Here are three warning signs that mean it is time to consider new ways of working to manage your multi-project assignments.

1 Your manager keeps giving you more work

You do regular reporting, and maybe even timesheets. You believe your manager knows what you are doing every day and how much work you have, so they are only giving you what they feel you should be able to do.

If your manager keeps giving you more work without discussion, that's a warning sign because often your manager hasn't got the capacity to track what you are doing day-to-day. They probably only have a very high-level overview of what you are working on. I guarantee they aren't studying your timesheet in detail every week and committing to memory the tasks that you have been working on.

> On one project, my sponsor asked me to take on a time-consuming admin task that (in my opinion) could have been done by one of the executive assistants or a temp. I couldn't get that done and my own workload, and I spoke – rather emotionally – to my manager about it. She explained that the project sponsor wouldn't know what else I was working on, so wouldn't have considered the possibility that I might not be able to get it done.
>
> Our project team was made up of senior managers. Despite speaking to my sponsor every day, the reality was I was expected to be able to manage my time and have grown-up conversations about workload if I needed to. Instead of doing that, I was burning out trying to please everyone.

Project sponsors are senior leaders who also have high workloads, often in a complex environment with many pressures that you may not be aware of. However much they try to understand what's going on, they can't know everything, especially if they are only responsible for part of your workload. In a multi-project environment where you are working for several leaders, the only one who knows exactly what your workload includes is you.

You're not alone if you feel like the amount of work coming from your manager is unsustainable. In a survey for this book, 44 per cent of project professionals reported that their manager giving them more work was a challenge, as you can see in Figure 2.2.

FIGURE 2.2   Major challenges of managing multiple projects

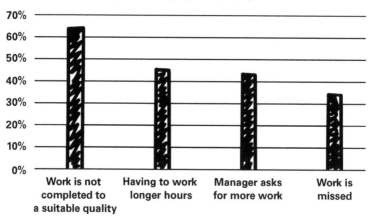

The first step in dealing with a situation where you keep being given more work is to fully map out what your current workload is. Chapter 3 will help you do that. Share this information with your manager and work together to assess the priorities.

Weekly, transparent, reporting on fast-moving projects also helps, and it should include the effort you are making as the project manager. For too long I reported on what the team was doing without including my tasks. Find ways to tell people what you are doing to raise the visibility of how you are spending your time.

2 You are working longer hours

When you get given more projects to run, sometimes it feels like the only way to get the work done is to spend more time at work. This is a warning sign because that's the start of the fast route to burnout. Nearly half of project managers (46 per cent) reported that they are working longer and longer hours as time goes by.

Project work has peaks and troughs of effort. However much you aim for a steady cadence to your work, there are issues that need to be resolved, last-minute changes and client requests: that's part of the role. There are also times when you will work longer hours to support your team. I remember staying late one evening just to be around while my IT colleagues were doing something critical for our project. I wasn't needed, but I felt like I wanted to be there for solidarity, and to show I recognized their efforts at working into the evening.

I also choose to get into the office and be the first one on my floor of the building from time to time, because I enjoy the peace and being able to ease myself into the day before the pace picks up. This means travelling at a time when I can get a seat on the train with no problems, and I am grateful for that too. While that works for me, watch out for feeling like you have to start early, finish late or fire up your laptop when you get home. That's a sign that you should be critically looking at your workload to make sure you have used all your strategies for structuring, combining, streamlining and batching your work to speed up how long it takes to do things.

In other words, if it takes ten hours a week to manage one project, it doesn't necessarily take 20 hours a week to manage two. Working efficiently between several projects is the best way to get the work done and get home on time. Throughout this book you will find tips and processes for how to do this. Use the right strategies to structure your work and manage your time, so you can take advantage of the dynamics and interactions between projects and processes.

> I routinely work on all the small projects (under $5 million value) in the office. There are many of them and it is easy to hand them over to me because I take them and run with it. Many of them are similar in scope and it can be hard to keep track of what project is specifically

doing what. Ultimately, the projects get done (and done well in my opinion) but it can be frustrating and stressful balancing scopes and schedules when they are all small but require a similar effort as the larger projects that a person may be tasked with only one or two of. Higher management doesn't necessarily see it that way which makes it frustrating. In the future, I would like to be able to say 'No' when asked to add one more 'small' project onto my plate.

Anonymous project manager

3 Work is slipping through the cracks

When you have a lot on the go at once, you need solid systems to make sure nothing is overlooked. Having said that, it's possible that even with the best systems in the world, something falls through the cracks from time to time. Ideally, that should be an unusual occurrence, rather than something that happens on a regular basis. As Figure 2.2. shows, about a third of project managers (34 per cent) report that work is slipping through the cracks and that's a challenge for them as a professional who is leading multiple projects.

If you feel like you are dropping balls more times than would like, consider how much your environment is setting you up for success. Are your systems really working for you? Are you taking a reactive approach to work, perhaps only working on something when someone asks for an update? That can result in a knee-jerk reaction like firing off some emails just to say that you're making progress. If you find yourself doing work in response to the last person who asked you for something, and being more reactive than feels comfortable, then consider that as a warning sign that you need to get on top of your tasks.

The good news is that you are in the right place: this book is going to help. Chapter 7 has tips for standardizing processes and creating checklists to help you manage your work in efficient ways.

Where to go from here

If you have recognized your workload and some of the challenges you face in these pages, then you may have come to the realization that it is worth trying different approaches for managing your projects because there could be better ways of using your existing skills and making your environment work for you. It honestly doesn't have to be so hard.

Keep an open mind as you move through the book and consider trying some of the activities, tools and techniques to see how much of an impact they could have on your efficiency levels – and the enjoyment you get from your work.

KEY TAKEAWAYS

- A multi-project environment naturally includes more moving parts: people, processes and products.

- Managing multiple projects requires a slightly different take on the core skills needed to deliver successful projects.

- Projects can form part or all of your workload.

- Watch out for warning signs that signal your current workload management techniques are becoming inefficient due to the volume of projects you are leading.

ACTION STEPS

Your action steps from this chapter are to:

- Identify what category your workload fits into. Do you have a sushi, spaghetti or side dish project workload? Or perhaps a blend of a categories?

- Reflect on your current position. Do you spot any of the warning signs? If you are a team leader, can you spot the warning signs in anyone in your team?

References

Anderson, C (2019) Welcome to the project economy, *LinkedIn*, 26 September. Available from: www.linkedin.com/pulse/welcome-project-economy-cindy-anderson-cae/ (archived at https://perma.cc/M6FM-HTQU)

Harrin, E (2021) Managing multiple projects: The research, 29 October. Available from https://rebelsguidetopm.com/managing-multiple-projects-the-research (archived at https://perma.cc/73XE-MV4Z)

Rezvani, A and Khosravi, P (2020) Critical success and failure factors in large-scale complex projects, in Phillips, M (2020) *The Practitioner's Handbook of Project Performance: Agile, waterfall and beyond*, Routledge, Abingdon

Schoper, Y, Wald, A, Ingason, H T and Fridgeirsson, T V (2018) Projectification in Western economies: A comparative study of Germany, Norway and Iceland, *International Journal of Project Management*, 36 (1), 74–82 (January)

Further reading

Williams, T C (2017) *Filling Execution Gaps: How executives and project managers turn corporate strategy into successful projects*, Walter de Gruyter, Boston

03

Concept #1: Portfolio: understanding your workload

The majority of project managers run between two and five projects at any one time (Harrin, 2021a). However, 15 per cent of project managers reported running over ten projects simultaneously. On top of a project workload, most employees have other tasks to do that do not fall within the boundaries of a project or an actual day job beyond managing projects. That's a lot of activities to fill your time.

The number of projects you are asked to lead depends on a wide variety of factors. Research by Kuprenas et al (2000) shows that prior experience is the factor that most influences the workload for a project manager. From that, we can conclude that if you have shown yourself to be a safe pair of hands running multiple projects in the past, you will likely be asked to take on a multi-project workload in the future. Complexity is another factor that influences workload: the same research also shows that project managers tend to get fewer highly complex projects. That means you may have a couple of high cost, high complexity projects or a larger number of low cost, low complexity projects. What is it for you?

The first concept covered by the framework for managing multiple projects is to create a personal portfolio, as shown in Figure 3.1. This is a summary statement of your work in list form that documents everything you are currently responsible for. The portfolio is important because before you can structure and streamline your work, you need to know exactly what that work looks like. The action of creating a personal portfolio serves three purposes:

1 It gives you the full picture of what is on your To Do list.
2 It provides clarity about what is expected of you.
3 It creates the information you need to communicate about your workload with other people.

FIGURE 3.1   The Portfolio concept in the managing multiple projects framework

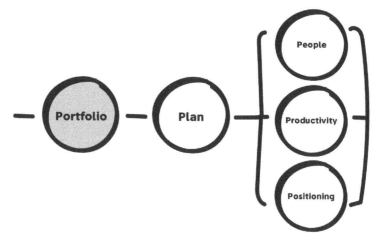

This chapter gives you the tools to understand and prioritize your workload, which is the foundation for being able to effectively prioritize time and make smarter decisions about how to consolidate some of your project management activity. You'll learn what portfolio management is and how you can use the principles of portfolio thinking to run your To Do list like a portfolio manager.

What is portfolio management?

The seventh edition of the *APM Body of Knowledge* (2019) defines a portfolio as 'a collection of projects and/or programmes used to structure and manage investments at an organizational or functional level to optimize strategy benefits or operational efficiency'. In other words, a portfolio is a way to group, structure and oversee the project-related work being undertaken across the organization or functional area, so that the highest value, most beneficial work takes priority. For example, an IT portfolio would list all the projects, programmes and larger pieces of operational work that the IT department is working on at any given moment in time. It could also include information about projects that are going through the approval process or waiting to start, along with any pieces of work that are currently on hold. The portfolio is the whole picture of the work for the team, usually as it relates to delivering change.

In practice, portfolios can take many forms. A portfolio can be:

- A collection of related work, for example work to do with a particular department.
- A collection of unrelated projects where it is helpful to manage them together, for example the portfolio for a whole organization, where projects happening in different departments do not necessarily relate to each other, but management wants visibility of all the work that is happening across the organization.

The benefit of thinking about work in this cohesive, combined way is that you can use the big picture to make better decisions. Portfolio management is that decision-making effort: it describes the work involved in managing a portfolio, including the choices that get made about the projects. It's a common concept within the world of strategy execution and project delivery because it allows for comparisons and rankings between projects based on different factors like priority, risk, cost, the effort involved and the amount of time the work will take (Durbin and Doerscher, 2010). You also have to make choices about how to invest your time and effort, so portfolio management lends itself well to thinking about your own workload too.

According to Reiss and Rayner (2013) the term 'portfolio management' has two interpretations:

- A management layer: the people responsible for the selection and delivery of any changes, projects or programmes within the organization.

- A process: the decision steps and workflow for choosing what gets done in what order.

As an individual managing a number of projects, the management layer aspect of portfolio management is simply you, and perhaps your direct manager or the people who assign you work. You may have a greater or lesser influence over the work you are asked to do. A small business owner will have a larger influence over the selection of projects to do because those choices are within their personal control. An employee will have less of a say about what they work on because those decisions are typically made by the hierarchical levels of management above them.

The process aspect is where you will have greater control: ultimately, you can decide how to spend your time each day and how you organize your work to combine activities to give you the best results.

Portfolio thinking

Managing a portfolio requires a specific way of thinking: a joined up, holistic way of looking at everything with a view to creating balance, assessing priorities and making choices. At an organizational level, portfolio thinking is shaped and constrained by what the Praxis Framework (undated) defines as the seven components of portfolio management:

1 Establishing an infrastructure to support projects and programmes.

2 Defining management procedures and processes to be used consistently across projects and programmes.

3 Optimizing the allocation of available resources by managing supply and demand.

4 Maintaining a portfolio that balances strategic objectives in changing conditions.

5 Improving the delivery of projects and programmes through a co-ordinated view of risk, resources, dependencies and schedules.

6 Co-ordinating the need for change with the capacity of the organization to absorb change.

7 Reducing costs by removing overlapping and poorly performing projects and programmes.

These elements reflect how an organization would want to structure its governance processes to ensure the right projects get done at the right time, with the right resources to deliver the right outcomes and benefits.

However, you can use portfolio thinking at an individual level too. By reframing these organizational responsibilities to make them applicable to your personal workload, you can structure your workload to look at it in a portfolio way, which will help you feel more in control: many of my students and mentees feel more confident once they can 'get their hands around the work' and brain dump all the projects and tasks that are taking up space in their heads. Portfolio thinking helps you see the connections between projects and activities that may make more sense if they are managed together.

The six principles of portfolio thinking at an individual workload level are shown in Figure 3.2 and are as follows:

1 Understand the big picture: all the tasks, projects and programmes in the portfolio.

2 Prioritize the work.

3 Group tasks and projects into buckets to make them easier to manage, monitor and control.

4 Plan and carry out all the work, and monitor progress against your plan.

5 Communicate project status and providing recommendations for actions to your manager, project sponsors and other key stakeholders.

6 Look for opportunities to continuously improve by learning as you go.

FIGURE 3.2   Six principles of portfolio thinking

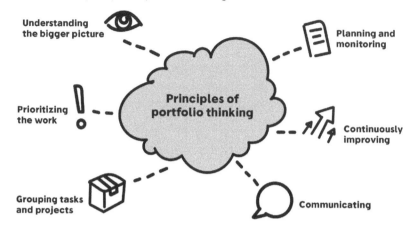

The first principle requires you to have a full understanding of what makes up your workload today. That big picture view will give you the contents of your personal portfolio and the foundation for creating efficient working practices. We will come back to the other principles as we go through the book.

Tasks, projects and programmes

Regardless of whether you have a sushi, spaghetti or side dish workload (see Chapter 2), it will be made up of tasks, projects and (sometimes) programmes.

A task is a piece of work assigned by someone to you or to someone else, often by a certain date. They are one-off, small(ish) activities that do not require the structure of a project management approach to manage them. In other words, you don't have to spend much time breaking down the work into smaller sections, planning it all out and following a governance process to make sure it's done the right way. Normally, you can do a task by yourself. Examples include:

· Preparing a slide deck;

· Booking a meeting venue;

· Emailing a proposal to a client.

Robert Wysocki (2019) came up with my favourite definition of a project: a 'sequence of unique, complex and connected activities that have one goal or purpose and that must be completed by a specific time, within budget, and according to specification'.

Projects are made up of lots of different tasks. The decision about whether a group of tasks is a project often comes down to whether you would benefit from using a structured approach to control and manage the work so that it gets done at the right time, by the right people, in the most efficient way. That structured approach is project management. Adopting project management practices, tools and techniques is the most effective way to ensure the work is carried out efficiently and to the correct standard.

You can only do the smallest projects by yourself. Normally, projects need input from other subject matter experts and team members, even if they only contribute on a part-time basis. Examples include:

- Launching a new product;
- Upgrading an IT application;
- Making improvements to a process based on customer feedback;
- Constructing a structure, like a house or a road.

A programme is 'a group of related projects that often use a similar group of resources and will together achieve an overall common objective or set of related objectives' (Harrin, 2018). In practice, a programme will often include tasks that don't neatly fit into a project and the goal is to deliver an outcome or benefit that relates to the organization's strategic objectives. It's often a transformative initiative. Programme teams are made up of a range of specialists, project managers and other stakeholders. Examples include:

- Digitizing the back office functions in a business;
- Transforming organizational culture;
- Moving to environmentally sustainable ways of working across the organization.

Create your personal portfolio

It's time to take the first steps in applying portfolio thinking to your workload. Using the principle of understanding the big picture, you are going to create a detailed list of what you are working on. The easiest way to do this is in a spreadsheet, but if you feel more comfortable recording the information in another format, such as mindmapping or another tool, then do so. Your goal is to document everything that currently forms part of your workload. List out the projects.

For each project, include the following information:

- Unique reference: to make it easier to talk about your list later;
- Project name: a short, descriptive title for the work;
- Status: in progress, not started, on hold. Don't include work that is complete;
- Priority: high, medium or low. If you have not been told the priority, ask someone or use your judgement and knowledge or organizational objectives to work it out (there are tools for prioritization covered later in this chapter);
- Sponsor or customer name;
- Department, client or group that the project is for;
- Objectives: one or two key points about the purpose of the project or what it is for;
- Forecasted completion date: your estimate of when the project will be finished or the date by which you have been asked to have the project complete;
- Deliverables: two or three of the major things this project will create;
- Dependencies: if you are already aware of dependencies between projects, note them here (there is more on dependencies in Chapter 4);
- Estimated hours per week: record how long you think you are or will be spending on this project in hours.

The result will be something like Table 3.1.

TABLE 3.1 Template for a personal portfolio workload tracking spreadsheet

| | | | | | | | | Expected completion | | | Hours per week |
| | | | | | | My workload | | | | | |
Project ID	Name	Status	Priority	Sponsor	Group	Objectives	date	Deliverables	Dependencies	(approx)
1001	Project X	In progress	Medium	[name]	IT	Point 1 Point 2 Point 3	[date]	Deliverable 1 Deliverable 2	Project Y	5
1002	Project Y	Not started	High	[name]	Engineering	Point 1 Point 2	[date]	Deliverable 1 Deliverable 2 Deliverable 3	None	15

Delegates on my training courses often find estimating hours per week is the hardest part of this process, especially if your organization does not mandate timesheets and you have nothing much to go on beyond your best guess. Your best guess is fine. Projects are typically busier at the beginning as you get things set up, before they fall into a comfortable rhythm, and then they require more project management effort again towards the end as the team prepares to handover the deliverables and close out the work. Your per-week hourly estimate doesn't have to be perfect or reflect those ebbs and flows in your workload. It's simply a guide for sizing to give you an idea about whether the project is taking up a lot of your time or not very much at all. It can also help you later with prioritizing your time and can indicate to your manager (if you share the information with them) just how busy you really are. If you really struggle with estimating hours, use T-shirt sizing instead: is it an extra small, small, medium, large, extra large or extra extra large piece of work? This is a way to measure project size relative to the other things on the list. Too many XXL projects running at the same time will be challenging to manage, but it may be OK to have one alongside a handful of small and medium-sized pieces of work.

The spreadsheet needs to work for you, so if it helps to break down a project into large pieces and consider it in chunks, then do so. However, it is not a project schedule, so it's not necessary to include every task on there.

> It makes sense to align your priority categorization with that of your organization. If the company standard is to assign priority on a different basis to high, medium or low, then use that as the way to allocate a priority to each of the items of your personal portfolio.

Non-project work

Even if you have the job title and role responsibilities of a project manager, it's unlikely that you spend 100 per cent of your time on project work. Everyone has other tasks to do that should also to be accounted for in your available time. After you have listed the projects in your workload tracking spreadsheet, add any additional non-project tasks that are taking up a regular amount of time.

Common tasks for people leading projects that are not actually project-related include:

- Organizing team meetings, team building or social events;
- Mentoring others or buddying new starters;
- Facilitating meetings or workshops for colleagues;
- Attending one-to-one meetings or performance reviews with your manager;
- Line management and recruitment for direct reports if you have them;
- Updating or creating templates, other process-related documentation and policies;
- Being responsible for organizational learning, for example organizing training for the team, hosting lunch-and-learn sessions or facilitating knowledge sharing in some way or your own professional development;
- Providing input to team or departmental strategy, working groups or committees.

You might find these tasks on sticky notes, in your task management app, as open items in your inbox or written in a notebook. Add them to your list, or perhaps group them into an entry for 'other' with a portion of your time allocated against them. When your portfolio list is complete, the spreadsheet is useful to help you spot whether there are any overlaps or conflicts between your projects, and as the starting point for seeing your workload as a personal portfolio.

> I filled out the spreadsheet for the major projects I was working on to help me prioritize. It was good to see the four or five big projects that I was running, and then the time I allocated to them per week.
>
> Omar Warrack, supply chain project manager, UK

Prioritizing the work

The second principle of personal portfolio management is to prioritize the work. But everything is a priority, right? While you might hear that from colleagues or managers, it can't be true – and even if it was, it's unrealistic to expect project managers to work on everything all at the same time. That's not how work works. Having said that, if you only worked on the project that is your top priority, you would never make any progress on projects that appear lower down the list. There is a balancing act in ensuring your priority projects get more of your time but the lower priority projects still get some attention – because no doubt your boss expects those to be moved on at least a little instead of ignored each month.

When work is identified in your portfolio spreadsheet, the next step is to prioritize it. Knowing the priority of your projects, and the priority of tasks within your projects, lets you make informed decisions about where to spend your time. Ideally, your project sponsors or your manager will help you to identify the priority work on your list. However, if they are unable (or unwilling) to do so, it is up to you to establish the relative priority of what you are working on so that you can effectively manage your own time.

There are a lot of different ways to do that. In a survey for this book (Harrin, 2021b), 30 per cent of project managers reported using more than one way to prioritize, so it is OK to use different techniques in different situations. Popular methods for prioritizing work include:

- The Eisenhower matrix (42 per cent reported using this);
- MoSCoW (20 per cent reported using this);
- ICE (18 per cent reported using this).

If you are wondering what those techniques are, they are explained in more detail below. However, it is interesting to note that 14 per cent of respondents relied on their professional judgement in an informal way, either by making their own priority-based To Do lists or by using upcoming deadlines from their project schedules. The 3 per cent of project managers who said they had no way to prioritize were probably doing something similar to get through the day. Some of the verbatim comments about how people prioritize included:

- It's often 'gut feeling' or management determination based on project constraints.
- Projects are aligned to company business objectives so identifying which objective is top priority for the business at this time and working from there.
- Whoever yells the loudest? (It's horrible and embarrassing to admit, I know!)
- Common sense and project dates.
- I have a regular scheduled meeting with the Managing Director to set priorities.
- Nothing structured. Mostly I use my timelines to determine key activities to prioritize. However, anything my manager asks for gets done first.
- When is their go live? And are they on track or how far off?
- Literally, it is whatever is on fire today.

Do you prioritize whatever is on fire? While sometimes you might have to, let's look at four ways to take a more structured approach to prioritizing work: MoSCoW, the Eisenhower matrix, ICE scoring and COST.

Putting projects into a priority order helps you think about how much time and effort to spend on each one, but in practice you will be spending time on all your projects. While you wait for a decision on a high priority project, you can be moving a lower priority piece of work forward. Use the gaps in higher priority projects to work to focus on other tasks.

MoSCoW

MoSCoW is a prioritization technique usually used for project requirements. Initially developed by Dai Clegg (Clegg and Barker,

1994), it was later adopted by the Dynamic Systems Development Method, an agile project delivery framework managed by the DSDM Consortium (now the Agile Business Consortium).

MoSCoW stands for:

- Must have;
- Should have;
- Could have;
- Won't have this time.

The additional letter o's don't stand for anything but they make the technique easier to say.

Typically, project teams use MoSCoW to prioritize work within a project and create a set of requirements. It's a way of defining project scope and setting expectations about what is most important and what's going to get delivered.

A slightly adapted version of MoSCoW can be used to prioritize work across your personal portfolio. In this multi-project version, MoSCoW stands for:

- Must do;
- Should do;
- Could do;
- Won't do at the moment.

The **must do** tasks are the projects and activities that are essential. If you don't do them, you might as well hand in your resignation. Perhaps they are codified in your job description, or they represent strategically important work for your department.

The **should do** projects are important, but they are not critical. If you don't take responsibility for completing that work, someone else is going to have to, or the organization will need to find a painful workaround to fill the gap.

The **could do** projects are initiatives that you will complete if you have the time. It will be considered a shame if they don't get done, but the pain level of not completing them is not as high as a 'should do' project. These might be good projects to delegate to a colleague with less experience than you, if the work is straightforward.

The **won't do** tasks are items in the portfolio that you will not work on at the moment. You make the decision to put those to one side, in order to free up time for more important work. You may come back and work on them later, but, for now, you don't need to do them – and neither does anyone else. The organization will not suffer for having to wait for them to be complete. These tasks can wait.

Priority is relative, so a project's priority will change based on what else is on your To Do list. The exercise of prioritization reflects the position at the time you rank your projects. A project that is low priority, not considered strategic or in your won't do list may become more important in a couple of months. Make time to reflect regularly on your prioritization decisions so you can move projects around as necessary and ensure you don't overlook something that is becoming more and more important.

Eisenhower matrix

The Eisenhower matrix (also known as the Eisenhower box, the Eisenhower decision principle or the urgent/important matrix) is named after Dwight D. Eisenhower, 34th President of the United States. It's not known if he used this prioritization method himself, but he referenced the basic concept which developed into the matrix in an address at the Second Assembly of the World Council of Churches in 1954.

In the speech, he quoted a former college president as saying, 'I have two kinds of problems, the urgent and the important. The urgent are not important, and the important are never urgent' (Eisenhower, 1954). From that basic idea that a task or project can have urgency or importance (or both – unlike his quote), the Eisenhower matrix was born.

The matrix is a two-by-two grid where one axis represents the urgency of the work and the other represents the importance of the work. Consider each of the four quadrants in relation to your projects and establish where they best fit. The four options are:

- High urgency, high importance. For example, tasks like:
  - Dealing with a crisis or issue;
  - Upcoming deadlines.
- Low urgency, high importance. For example, tasks like:
  - Relationship-building activities;
  - Developing strategy and forward-looking plans;
  - Projects that contribute to strategy but don't have any delivery dates or milestones in the near future;
  - Identifying new opportunities;
  - Team or personal and professional development activities.
- High urgency, low importance. For example, tasks like:
  - Responding to incoming messages where the expectation is that you will reply quickly;
  - Dealing with a full inbox;
  - Talking to a colleague who has shown up at your desk;
  - Being asked to attend meetings at short notice.
- Low urgency, low importance. For example, tasks like:
  - Projects that are not due to start for several months;
  - Time-wasting activities such as social media where this is not part of your job or being interrupted.

I was approached in the office by a senior manager who asked me to attend a meeting that was happening at that moment. I had not been invited before this moment, did not know what the meeting was about or how I was expected to contribute, and, of course, I had nothing prepared. In their opinion, the meeting was important; for me, it was less important as it was an interruption to my day. However, it was urgent as it needed to happen straight away.

The Eisenhower matrix can be used for prioritizing the work in your personal portfolio, although it is more commonly used for individual tasks instead of projects. When using it to prioritize projects, consider the timeline for the work. Projects with high proximity – the closer the expected completion date – have higher urgency. The more strategically-aligned or essential the work is considered by your manager, the higher up it should appear on the importance axis and the more of your attention it should command.

When using the matrix to prioritize tasks, be extremely critical about where you put each activity. Work that might feel important because it takes up a lot of time may not be getting you closer to your goals. For example, a study by Carleton University (Duxbury and Lanctot, 2017) found that people spent one-third of their time reading and answering emails, but 30 per cent of the time those emails are neither urgent nor important. In an eight-hour working day, that's about 48 minutes spent on emails that don't really matter.

ICE scoring

ICE stands for impact, confidence and ease. ICE scoring is a concept developed and made popular by Sean Ellis (2015), founder of GrowthHackers. Originally for internal use to help prioritize business growth experiments and tests, it can be used as a decision-making tool to prioritize almost anything.

Score each project on your portfolio spreadsheet out of ten for the following characteristics:

- Impact: If this project completes successfully, what will be the impact on the organization, corporate objectives, the department, your career and so on?
- Confidence: How certain are you that this project can be completed successfully with the knowledge, data and experience that you have?
- Ease: How easy do you think it will be to do this project with the time and resources that you have?

The ICE score is the average of the three individual scores and gives each of your projects a rating from one to ten.

As an example, let's say you've been asked to lead a project to organize an event to celebrate 20 years of your company being in business. You know the project will have a high impact for your community and you are confident that you can host the event successfully, as the organization has done similar events several times before, even though it's your first time as project manager. You're juggling several other projects so it won't necessarily be easy to fit the work in but you give it scores of seven for impact, nine for confidence and six for ease. The ICE score for this project is seven. That information helps you prioritize the project among your other work.

COST

Finally, let me share an approach I use personally. The COST model is a simple way of prioritizing projects by the value they offer the company. COST stands for compliance, operations, strategic and tactical. Projects are categorized into those four groups and then they can be worked on in that order.

Compliance projects are initiatives that ensure the organization meets regulatory and compliance requirements. If these projects were not done, the organization would have to cease operations. Examples include:

- Changing processes to meet new regulatory requirements.
- Carrying out the work required to meet an external audit or industry assessment.
- Updating and configuring software and hardware to meet new legal standards for data protection.

If you have any projects in your portfolio that fit into the compliance category, they should be your top priority.

Operations projects are those designed to keep the company operational and meeting its requirements to customers. Think of these projects as the ones that 'keep the lights on'. If these projects were not done, the organization would cease to be viable longer term. Customers would leave and products and services would not be maintained. Examples include:

- Technical software and hardware upgrades to ensure the IT estate is fit for purpose and remains within service contracts.
- Process improvements to address issues with customer support.
- Procuring a fleet of vehicles to replace old vehicles that are end-of-life.

Operations projects are your next priority because, without them, the organization's viability is at risk.

Strategic projects help the organization turn its strategic plan into reality. Projects are how organizations deliver strategy and get the business closer to its goals. If these projects were not done, the company would fail to deliver on its strategic plan. Examples include:

- Launching a new product or service;
- Improvements that relate to cost savings;
- Initiatives with the aim of improving customer or employee satisfaction.

While strategic projects might sound like they are top priority, they actually rank third in this model. This group of projects is normally work to do with making change and improvements. Note that compliance projects and operations projects would also be mentioned on a company's strategic plan. Staying in business and meeting regulatory requirements would be a key part of any organizational strategy, although they might not routinely make the Town Hall briefings or 'top projects for the year' presentations. However, we split out those compliance and operations projects and use the strategic category for work that is of strategic importance but does not qualify as compliance or operations.

Tactical projects are everything else, typically discretionary improvements that would be nice to have but that don't take priority over the other categories. These projects have been recognized as good ideas but don't have to be implemented right now. If the projects are not done, there's no substantive impact. However, today's tactical project can become tomorrow's strategic project, as business needs change over time, so it is always worth revisiting your prioritization on a regular basis to check your categorization remains correct. Examples include:

- Acting on comments from the employee suggestions scheme;
- User-suggested software enhancements that don't affect functionality;
- Process improvements.

These are the lowest level of priority for you and – if you have projects that fit into any of the other categories – should be timetabled to take up the least of your time.

In summary, you are aiming to prioritize the work that makes the most impact and offers the most value balanced against the time, budget and effort it will take to achieve it. It's not an exact science. You can choose any of the techniques above, something else entirely, or a blend of methods. Most managers will be open to listening to why you have prioritized the projects the way you have, as long as you can explain your thinking. The important part is putting in the time to reflect on what each project involves so you can include priority in your personal portfolio.

How many priority projects is too many?

There is no specific number of priority projects that you should have; no number beyond which your workload becomes unmanageable. In their book, *Not Today*, Erica and Mike Schultz (2021) suggest that you forget about thinking in absolute numbers and instead consider the following factors for each project on your list:

- How much time will it take?
- How big a change is it?
- How uncertain is the outcome?

- How much emotional energy will it require?
- What resources will it take?

It might be manageable to take on another priority project if it's only going to last a few days. A large organizational change project that requires making many people redundant will impact your emotional energy as well as take up a lot of change management time. Projects with a high degree of uncertainty typically need more attention than those with a tried-and-tested plan.

Review your answers: trust your intuition if you look at the list and feel what you see is too many 'top' priorities. If that is the case, start the conversation with your manager about how to deprioritize some of your work in order to focus on what truly is the most important work.

Group the work

The third principle of personal portfolio management is grouping the work. If you can group the work into buckets, it becomes less overwhelming and you benefit from efficiencies of managing things together. We'll look at techniques for managing activities together later in the book. For now, focus on looking for connections between the things on your portfolio list. Here are some ways that you can group.

- By stakeholder: Do you have common resources or subject matter experts who are working with you on multiple projects? Perhaps you have multiple projects for the same sponsor, department, customer or client.
- By theme or content: Do your projects have common deliverables or subject matter? For example, group all the projects that you're doing that involve construction, or the projects that involve web design.
- By location: Do your projects serve a particular geographic location? Can you split them by country or region?

- By lifecycle stage: Do you have multiple projects going through a common project process in the lifecycle? You could group all your projects that are in the initiation phase, for example, so that you can work on common activities for them all.

- By project management approach: Do you have projects using different approaches? Maybe you've got some that are using a waterfall or predictive methodology, and others where you're working in a more iterative way following agile methods.

- By amount of active management required: Do you have some projects where you have to be very hands-on and a lot of active management is required? And others where you can be more hands-off as the team knows what is expected of them? Cluster your projects by the amount of management effort you need to spend on them.

- By deadline: Do you have projects that share a common end date? It could be advantageous to group them together. For example, look at all the projects due to complete in the next quarter.

- By software: Do you run projects using a range of different software tools? This can happen when clients ask you to use their tools and, as the project manager, you end up having project data split across a number of applications. There are time-savings to be had by going in and updating everything in one system at the same time.

If none of these feels like natural groupings for your work, look for any other connections between projects so that you can make your buckets. Give each bucket a descriptive name like 'IT Projects', 'Client X's Projects' or 'Due by year-end' so you know what the group represents. These names are for your personal use to help you refer to them later, so don't worry about them too much.

The number of buckets you end up with will depend on the original number of projects on your list. The more buckets you have, the harder it will be to see any tangible improvements from managing your workload as a portfolio. Three to five buckets would be a reasonable result; if you end up with more it could be worth looking over your list again to see what other similarities you can find to further consolidate the list. It doesn't matter how many individual projects fall into each bucket: some might have many, another may have just one project.

It's not a problem if you end up with fewer than three buckets. You may be able to manage your entire portfolio in a way that consolidates everything. However, as you start to use the combined approaches to managing your work, you may find you do need to split out certain aspects. Stay flexible and be prepared to make changes until you find a set of buckets that works well for you.

I have worked in multiple project management for more than ten years now. The hard thing is to keep the motivation. Not all projects are interesting, not all projects are passionating... To keep up, I need to find one new challenge, one new passion and new people to meet. Otherwise, it becomes simply boring. If we do not want to feel trapped like a rat in a cage running in a wheel, we need to look beyond the projects, and human interactions are the best solution to provide that shot of adrenaline.

Juan Manuel, EU projects officer, La Réunion

The portfolio as a communication tool

At this point, you will have a spreadsheet that contains a complete list of all your projects and additional repetitive tasks, all prioritized and organized into buckets. If you do nothing else after reading this book, this activity alone will help you gain clarity about what is expected of you and whether that is reasonable.

Your personal portfolio is a good communication tool to start a dialogue with your manager. Use it as part of a conversation about your current workload. Ask them if they agree with your prioritization. Bring out the list when you are asked to take on another project and have a discussion about what drops further down your list to make space for the new work.

KEY TAKEAWAYS

- A portfolio is a collection of projects or programmes.

- Portfolio thinking helps you identify connections between tasks and projects, taking a big picture view.

- Understanding your workload provides the foundation of your personal portfolio: the contents of which represents everything on your To Do list.

- Prioritization techniques like COST, MoSCoW, the Eisenhower matrix and ICE scoring enable you to identify the work that will make the most impact and offer the most value.

- Group your projects into logical buckets to maximize efficiencies in how they are managed.

ACTION STEPS

Your action step from this chapter is to create your personal portfolio. Here's how to do it.

- Create a workload spreadsheet (or equivalent) covering all the projects and major recurring tasks that you are working on.

- Prioritize the work on the list.

- Look for connections between projects and group similar work into logical buckets.

References

Agile Business Consortium (undated), Chapter 10: MoSCoW Prioritization. Available from www.agilebusiness.org/page/ProjectFramework_10_MoSCoWPrioritisation (archived at https://perma.cc/3MDV-LRCH)

Association for Project Management (2019) *APM Body of Knowledge*, 7th edn, APM, Princes Risborough

Clegg, D and Barker, R (1994) *CASE Method Fast-Track: A RAD approach*, Addison-Wesley, Boston

Covey, S (2018) *The 7 Habits of Highly Effective People*, Free Press, New York

Durbin, P and Doerscher, T (2010) *Taming Change with Portfolio Management: Unify your organization, sharpen your strategy, and create measurable value*, Greenleaf Book Group, Austin, Texas

Duxbury, L and Lanctot, A (2017) Carleton study finds people spending a third of job time on email. Available from newsroom.carleton.ca/archives/2017/04/20/carleton-study-finds-people-spending-third-job-time-email/ (archived at https://perma.cc/4SW8-A83X)

Eisenhower, D D (1954) Address at the Second Assembly of the World Council of Churches, Evanston, Illinois. August 19, 1954. Available from www.presidency.ucsb.edu/documents/address-the-second-assembly-the-world-council-churches-evanston-illinois (archived at https://perma.cc/5F5C-VZXL)

Ellis, S (2015) The Growth Team: How to build a high performance growth team. Available from www.slideshare.net/startupfest/startupfest-2015-sean-ellis-growthhackerscom-how-to-stage (archived at https://perma.cc/M6FY-MPXA)

Harrin, E (2018) *Project Manager*, BCS Learning & Development, Swindon

Harrin, E (2021a) The 2021 project management report, 22 March. Available from https://rebelsguidetopm.com/project-management-statistics/ (archived at https://perma.cc/DA3W-PKAP)

Harrin, E (2021b) Managing multiple projects: The research, 29 October. Available from https://rebelsguidetopm.com/project-management-statistics/ (archived at https://perma.cc/XG4F-XUKT)

Kuprenas, J A, Jung, C-L, Fakhouri, A S and Jreij, W G (2000) Project manager workload – assessment of values and influences, *Project Management Journal*, **31** (4), 44–51 (December)

Praxis Framework (undated) Project, Programme and Portfolio Management. Available from www.praxisframework.org/en/knowledge/project-programme-and-portfolio-management (archived at https://perma.cc/D7EQ-4VJ5)

Reiss, G and Rayner, P (2013) *Portfolio and Programme Management Demystified: Managing multiple projects successfully*, Routledge, Abingdon

Schultz, E and Schultz, M (2021) *Not Today: The 9 habits of extreme productivity*, BenBella Books, Dallas

Wysocki, R K (2019) *Effective Project Management: Traditional, agile, extreme, hybrid*, 8th edn, Wiley, Indianapolis

Further reading

Association for Project Management (2019) *Portfolio Management: A practical guide*, APM, Princes Risborough

Kendall, G I and Rollins, C (2003) *Advanced Project Portfolio Management and the PMO: Multiplying ROI at warp speed*, J Ross, Boca Raton

PMI (2017) *The Standard for Portfolio Management*, 4th edn, PMI, Newtown Square

04

Concept #2: Plan: Combining project schedules

Your personal portfolio and project prioritization will only get you so far. You've probably discovered from doing that exercise that you've got numerous pieces of work with overlapping timetables. Project scheduling involves creating a timetable for each project but, when you have a lot of projects, there's a risk that you miss seeing the big picture.

Resist the temptation to dive in and start clearing some of those timeline tasks from your To Do list. Before you get going on executing your plans, you need to take a moment to think strategically and understand the bigger picture. 'If you're too busy and frenzied to think', writes Dorie Clark (2021) in her book, *The Long Game*, 'then it's almost impossible to break out of a short-term mindset.'

The short-term mindset is what will keep you reacting to what is on your calendar for next week instead of looking forward. To do that, you need to create a more strategic vision for your work in the coming months: a consolidated, big picture view at a relatively high level that encompasses all your projects and allied work.

If that sounds like a challenge, then you are not alone. Rich Horwath, from the Strategic Thinking Institute, surveyed over 500 managers in 25 companies and concluded that the top strategy challenge is time: 96 per cent of people don't have enough time (or choose not to spend the time) on strategic thinking (Horwath, 2012).

The second concept in the managing multiple projects framework, as Figure 4.1 reminds us, is combining project schedules. In this chapter, we take a strategic approach to multi-project scheduling. You do need to find what Clark calls 'white space' to dedicate some time to completing this level of planning. But it will be worth it.

FIGURE 4.1   The Plan concept in the managing multiple projects framework

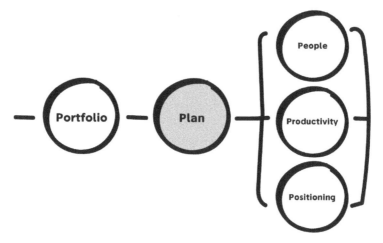

When you create a consolidated schedule for your projects, you can more easily predict when your busy times are going to be and where project timelines could clash. It can also show you where projects are dependent on each other and how to best make use of skilled people who are working on more than one of your projects, so they aren't overloaded. In other words, a consolidated timeline for your portfolio improves your ability to monitor and control the work.

Before you start scheduling

The fourth principle of personal portfolio management (as we saw in Chapter 3) is planning and carrying out the work, and monitoring progress against that plan, so schedules are required. The prerequisite for combining project schedules is that each project needs to have a schedule in the first place. You can't combine what doesn't exist! Go through your portfolio and check that every project has, as a minimum, a high-level timeline. It doesn't have to be detailed but you will need an idea of the key dates and milestones, as well as an idea of what resources (people and things) you need.

If you don't have enough information yet to be able to plan out the full timeline for any project, look at the section on rolling wave planning later in this chapter.

Project dependencies

The next step in creating a multi-project schedule is to look at the dependencies between your projects.

What is a dependency?

A dependency is a relationship that links the order in which tasks are carried out. Dependencies are how tasks are linked together or relate to each other.

On a single project schedule, you've probably seen this kind of thing on a Gantt chart before: the black lines show the flow of the work and the dependencies between the tasks, as shown in Figure 4.2. If you're familiar with Gantt charts, this will not be new to you.

Even if you don't use Gantt charts for scheduling your work, there are other ways of visually linking tasks. It might be typing the number of the successor or predecessor task into a list. It might be linking tasks on a Kanban board, or even using sticky notes for tasks and drawing lines between them to map out the flow of work in a project. It might be giving tasks the same reference number. However you record them, these dependencies are baked into the project schedule, and it's often pretty easy to manage them as project management software tools have the features required to link tasks in a variety of ways.

In a multi-project environment, the effort moves beyond linking activities in a single project to linking the relationships between

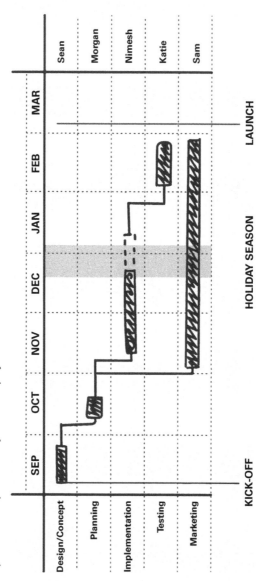

FIGURE 4.2   Dependencies represented by lines on a project timeline

projects. Projects may relate to each other in different ways, for example:

- Resource dependency: projects share human or other resources and this puts a constraint on when work can be done. For example, one subject matter expert needs to contribute to two projects but cannot be in two places at once, so their availability dictates the project timelines.

- Knowledge dependency: one project relies on the knowledge created by another. For example, one project trials a new technology which will then be used to build the deliverables for a second project.

- Task dependency: activities within projects are linked in some way. For example, a task on one project has to be completed before a task on another project can be started.

- Deliverable dependency: the output created by one project will be used as an input to another project. For example, a rebranding project creates new brand guidelines which are then used as an input to another project that has the objective of refreshing the company website.

Bilgin et al (2017) identify further relationships that exist within a portfolio of construction projects including financial dependencies, such as financial difficulties with a client affecting more than one project being completed for that client, and the fact that winning a new project may be dependent on successfully completing an existing project. Perhaps you can identify similar dependencies in your personal portfolio, even if you do not work in a construction environment.

You may be the project manager for each of the projects that relate, or your project may be providing knowledge, staff, tasks or deliverables to the work of another project manager. Either way, it's worth having a full understanding of inter-project dependencies as they can affect your ability to deliver the work successfully. Many enterprise project management tools will help you do that, for example by creating network diagrams that show interrelated projects. If you don't have software that will make it easy to show those relationships, below we look at two low-tech ways to give you enough information to adequately manage interactions between projects without having to be a pro planner or use new tools.

How to identify inter-project dependencies

If your portfolio is thematically linked, or you are working on a programme, you may have easy-to-spot dependencies between projects. For example, one project has to begin or finish before something can happen on another project. Perhaps a client has to approve something before another project can move forward. Sequence your projects by looking at how they relate to each other.

Once those easy connections have been identified, think about what else could affect the success of those projects. That could involve work happening on projects outside of your control. One of the largest areas for dependency management is people. It's common to have subject matter experts working on multiple projects so your project teams may include the same people. Look for where people are a dependency, because their availability will influence when work can be done.

Dependencies of any kind can affect the sequencing of the work. Knowing how your projects interrelate (within your own portfolio of work and with other project managers' work) will help you make smart choices about what to tackle first, and how to best make sure everyone is available to do the right tasks at the right time. When you dig into what your projects are delivering and how they are going to deliver those outputs, you may not find any dependency linkages between your projects, and that's fine. Knowing there are no dependencies is still useful information – and remember that as your projects evolve, that situation could change. New dependencies can crop up at any time.

Figure 4.3 shows an example of interproject dependencies recorded in a dependency map. Here, the planning phase of Project 1 is going to provide information or deliverables that will then be used to initiate Project 2. Next, something happens in the execution phase of Project 1 that has to be finished before Project 3 can be closed. Not

FIGURE 4.3   Example of a dependency map

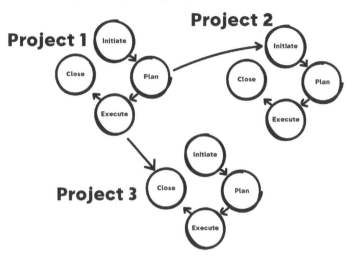

all projects will interlink in ways similar to this, but the majority of project managers in a multi-project environment do have to manage inter-project dependencies.

In a survey for this book (Harrin, 2021), 59 per cent of project managers reported leading work that was dependent on other projects they were running. Nearly 70 per cent of respondents said their projects had dependencies on other people's projects. It is also common to have to juggle both types of dependencies: 43 per cent of professionals said they handled a personal portfolio that required them to both manage dependencies between projects they were leading and those that others were leading. Only 16 per cent of people reported only running projects that had no dependencies on any other projects.

If your projects have dependencies on other work, a map like the one in Figure 4.3 gives you clarity about how projects depend on each other. That helps you see the bigger picture and make better decisions about how all of your work can be prioritized effectively and structured effectively. It can also prompt you to start conversations with people who rely on the outputs of your projects, or people on whom you are reliant in order to complete your work. Keep those communication channels open to maximize everyone's chances of getting what they need to finish their projects successfully.

Once you have identified the dependencies that affect the sequencing of your projects, it's important to document them in a way that allows the team to understand them and monitor them carefully. As with all things on projects, a situation can change. You may well find that what feels like an unimportant dependency now becomes critical later, or something shifts around and what wasn't a dependency now becomes something that you need to be aware of.

Documenting dependencies in a source and target matrix

There is no hard and fast rule for mapping project dependencies, and you can approach this task any way you like. You might have already started to record dependencies on the portfolio workload spreadsheet. One option is to put the links into a consolidated project schedule, showing the dependencies between projects on a Gantt chart.

However, dependency mapping between projects on a task-level view can soon get complicated. Another (simpler) option is to create a separate source and target matrix that shows how project activities relate to other projects, an example of which is shown in Table 4.1. The source and target matrix shows the project that is the source of the requirement or activity and the project that is the target recipient of that work. The matrix is a useful communication tool for explaining how projects relate to each other and why you've scheduled the work in a particular order.

> I used a dependency matrix for a group of several related projects. I inherently knew of the dependencies, but the value for me was having a way to document exactly how those projects were tied to each other. Reviewing the matrix with my team was also valuable because they could give input on ways to manage the dependencies, propose ideas about how they could actually help, and ensure overall project success.
>
> Robert Valle, senior project manager, USA

TABLE 4.1 Source and target matrix for identifying project dependencies

Project task dependencies

Source		Target			
Source	Project 1	Project 2	Project 3	Project 4	Project 5
Project 1		Documentation on tech solution			Copy of Policy X once it is written
Project 2				Expert resource being borrowed for Phase 2	
Project 3	Notification of time changes are taking place				Input to Phase 2 strategy
Project 4	Copies of training materials	Comms on the training so they can reuse it			
Project 5			Milestone 5 needs to be on time		

Keep dependencies up to date

The project environment is fluid, and that's even more the case in a multi-project environment. A project change, risk or issue can affect the dependencies on your source and target matrix, or it may create new dependencies. If you get a request for a change, use the matrix to identify if it would possibly impact other projects in your portfolio.

Consolidating your schedules

Project managers tend to live or die by their schedules. They shape decisions, priorities and stakeholder engagements. We feel good when the schedules give us confidence. We feel nervous when they change a lot. We feel out of control when the schedule is clearly fictional with no chance of ever being delivered. It's no surprise that scheduling can be such an emotional activity. According to Teresa Amabile and Stephen Kramer in their book, *The Progress Principle* (2011), there are three things that shape the positive feelings you have about work time: making meaningful progress, events that directly help project work and moments of positive interpersonal activity. Scheduling is all about making progress towards a meaningful goal so it's no wonder dates and deadlines play such an important part in whether work feels in or out of control.

Multi-project scheduling adds another layer to hitting deadlines. Instead of moving towards one meaningful goal, you are moving towards several at the same time. You've got several independent project schedules, whether they are detailed Gantt charts, task lists with dates, or timelines in some other format. Individually, they may all look manageable. But you aren't working on them individually. You have a multi-project portfolio to review and that means you need a big picture view of task deliverable dates so you can better organize your calendar.

Consolidating your schedules means you can predict when you will be busy. Look for overlapping periods of intense activity or where deliverables are due on several projects at the same time. These are days, weeks or months when your time will be stretched and it's helpful to know that before you find yourself in the middle of a work-load crisis. There are two ways to bring your schedules together:

- The ladder view
- The hot air balloon view.

The ladder view: a detailed schedule

Think of standing at the top of a ladder. You can see the ground quite clearly. You've got a full view of what's going on, and your view is made all the better from being up a little bit higher than you were at ground level. That's what we're aiming for with a detailed combined schedule. The ladder view schedule is useful for identifying:

- What needs to be done when across multiple projects from one plan.
- Potential resource conflicts where people are allocated to multiple projects at the same time.
- Busy points in the coming months so you can plan accordingly.
- Where activities can be merged to benefit the team, for example combining governance meetings (there is more on governance in Chapter 7).

The ladder view is also a useful tool for communicating about your projects and provides a visual overview of what's going on for you, your project sponsor and your team. Create the ladder view by taking all your project timelines and consolidating them into one document. If you use a Gantt chart, that means creating one 'master' Gantt chart that combines all your schedules.

Whatever tool you create it in, if you intend to use this schedule as your daily To Do list or work management tool, it's going to have to include everything: your own tasks as well as the tasks for the team. If you have a lot of projects and a lot of tasks in each project, that is going to shape up into a monster of a plan. As schedules change, you will have a lot of updates to do.

However, a slightly easier way to create a master schedule is to be selective about what makes it in. Only include the major phases of work, milestones and any tasks that span two reporting periods (as a rule of thumb, that makes a task long enough and significant enough to make it onto your consolidated schedule). You will have to maintain the detail in a separate schedule, alongside your ladder view plan. This should give you enough information to benefit from the economies of managing multiple projects together, but without the overwhelm of thousands of lines on your schedule.

The ladder view approach is suitable for portfolios where the vast majority of your work is related, there are a lot of dependencies between tasks and you use common resources. A detailed, consolidated schedule is also a useful communication tool with your team or project sponsor if all the work is relevant to them. Regardless of how thematically grouped your work is, if you feel putting all your project schedules in one document would be a better management approach and help you feel in control, then that is equally a good reason to do it.

> I work with multiple stakeholders and multiple projects all the time. Over the past year the number of projects has grown tremendously and initially I hit a brick wall after I got above ten projects. Microsoft Planner within Teams and Microsoft To Do were the game-changers for me. It helped clear my mind with a morning brain dump into the To Do. Then I would develop My Today tasks. When I got through My Today tasks, I focused in on longer range tasks, follow ups or weekly managerial requirements.
>
> Erac Priester, USA

The hot air balloon view: a high-level schedule

Now think of being up in a hot air balloon. You are higher than standing on a ladder so you can't see the ground quite so clearly. You can pick out the big features in the landscape: rivers, hills, roads, towns and clusters of industrial buildings. This is the view we're aiming for with a high-level schedule.

The hot air balloon schedule is useful for quickly identifying periods where multiple projects have deliverables or milestones due at the same time so you can plan accordingly. It is a roadmap for what's coming up and it gives you a big picture view with relatively little effort. Create this view of your work by looking at the schedules for each of your projects and picking out the milestones or major phases. Create a side-by-side list for all your projects using that information, like the example in Table 4.2. A table or spreadsheet works well for this: list the projects down the side, put months or quarters across the top (or even weeks, if your projects are short-term), and write in the major milestones where the columns and rows intersect for each project.

The benefit to this approach is that it is far less time-consuming than creating a detailed combined schedule. It highlights the busy times and gives you that hot air balloon view of your upcoming dead-lines. For example, in Table 4.2, the project manager will be very busy in February, with Project 1 going through testing, having to start the planning for Project 2 while facilitating requirements elicitation for Project 3 and closing down Project 4 at the same time.

This way of looking at your work is an overview; you still need to maintain an individual schedule for each project so that you have somewhere to track progress at a detailed level. It is also only a snap-shot of a single moment in time, as project schedules change. However, as a way to identify what's coming up so you can be prepared, the hot air balloon view is very helpful. It is also a great communications tool if you are trying to explain why you can't take on any more work or why perhaps you need to recruit extra people in your team in a way that a detailed task by task activity listing might be overwhelming for the person looking at that information.

This approach is best for projects that don't feel they would suit a fully combined, detailed master schedule. When your projects are unrelated, or your workload doesn't group into a single bucket, then the hot air balloon view shows you the big picture in a relatively low-effort way.

TABLE 4.2 Example of major project phases/events organized by month

Projects		Months				
	Jan	Feb	March	April	May	June
Project 1	Test	Test	Training	Go live at pilot location 1	Go live at pilot location 2	Pilot continues
Project 2	Business case	Planning	Planning	Design	Design	Design
Project 3	BAU	Requirements meeting	Focus groups	Proposal		Project begins
Project 4	Go live	Handover to operations	Lessons learned meeting			
Non-project work	Performance reviews					Half year reviews

Include additional tasks

Whether you go for the hot air balloon view or the ladder view, it is worth including any additional tasks from your portfolio spreadsheet that feel significant. Create a section or column in your plan for those additional tasks so they don't get lost. These are non-project responsibilities, but you don't want to lose sight of them so it is worth highlighting them because they can create busy times for you as well.

There is no hard and fast rule for whether the ladder view or the hot air balloon view is going to be best for you, but you probably have an instant feeling for which one would give you the best visibility and control. You can use one approach for certain projects and the other for the rest of your portfolio: mix and match as you see fit to give you the best visibility for the work that is to come.

Review your combined schedule

Once you have finished combining the project schedules together, take a look at what that has given you. Make sure that the inter-project dependencies you identified have been incorporated into the flow of the work, so you plan to work on the right things in the right order.

Ideally, you would prioritize your time on the most important project, and the schedule would reflect that. However, if you only worked on the priority projects, other projects wouldn't make any progress. If you can negotiate a pause on some of those lower priority items, then go for it! That will free up some time to speed ahead on priority work. However, for most people the reality is having to demonstrate progress in all projects, and keeping all stakeholders happy that their projects are moving forward, regardless of what priority they are in the big picture.

A good way to do that is to timebox your work based on the priority of the projects, so you're spending some time on each project every week or month, making sure that all your projects move forward even if just by a little bit. The impact of this on your schedule is that the lower priority projects have their timelines extended. You can make this adjustment on your combined schedule if it is within your authority to do so.

Prioritize between your projects first, using the information in your portfolio spreadsheet (and the source and target matrix if appropriate). Decide how much time to dedicate to each project per month. Allocate time in your calendar and on the schedule for each project based on the priority level.

Creating timeboxes to enable all projects to move forward is a technique that also works on a day-to-day basis. Look at your calendar for the week and make sure you are allocating more time to the top priority work but still leaving some time for other projects. When I made this change to my calendar planning, I allocated Monday and Tuesday for one project, one day for another project, a morning on another project, an afternoon on another project and a whole day on Friday for other things.

Yes, you'll get interrupted and there will be meetings booked at times that don't fit your plan. But if you start the week with the intention that you will work on each of your projects, then that helps you mentally approach time with the right prioritization in mind. The idea is that all of your projects move forward, but the priority projects get more of your focus time. Timeboxing is my favourite method for managing time across multiple projects.

Next, adjust the schedule for any known planned holidays or absences for you and the team. Some workplaces close over the end of year period, for example, and you could also have individuals with upcoming planned medical leave, parental leave and so on. Look at where those absences fall on the schedule and what impact they have.

Regardless of whether you chose a ladder view or a balloon view to visualize the entirety of your portfolio, one of the benefits of consolidating your project schedules is being able to see when your busy times are going to be.

Your combined schedule can be a useful communication tool for talking to your manager about your workload. It's a visual way of highlighting the impact of managing multiple projects and the expectations of project sponsors. If your combined schedule looks a little scary, use it to open the door to a conversation about changing some of the delivery dates for lower priority projects to allow you and the rest of the team the time to do the work to the best of your ability.

Sharing your combined schedule

Now you have a combined schedule, how can you use it for better communication? This is an important consideration if you have information in the schedule that is not relevant for everyone to see. The combined schedule is a personal document designed to help you more easily see how work fits together and when different activities are happening across your workload (there's more on planning for busy times below). You will want to share it with your manager and possibly your project sponsors.

However, there are groups of people for whom it would not be appropriate to see this information, for example external suppliers or clients who are not involved in all the projects represented on the schedule. If you need to communicate timelines and activities with them, it is better to create a separate version that only contains the information they need to see. They may still appreciate a consolidated version for all the projects they are working on with you, but they don't need to see any information relating to projects where they are not a part. Use individual action logs for each project (see 'Task-level planning' below) for detailed communication with external stakeholders, again, filtered as necessary by what is appropriate to share with them.

Tailoring the information shared with stakeholders also has the benefit of making it easier for them to understand. They won't be distracted by erroneous information as you are providing them with what they need to do their job.

Planning for busy times

Combining your timelines gives you advance warning of when intense periods of work will fall. So, what can you do with that information? The first consideration is whether those dates are in your control.

You may uncover data that show it could be advantageous or challenging to have the work scheduled at that time. For example, if you are implementing new software tools for the marketing team, it could be useful to have two projects launching together so you can consolidate the training and communication. Or you may be able to get the team leader to agree that would result in change overload for the users. Perhaps you could push out one project so that the team has a chance to get used to using one tool before having to learn the next, thus minimizing the impact of change fatigue.

Think about what you can influence to make the projects easier for you and other stakeholders. The reality for many people will be that they will not be able to influence project timelines as much as they would like, as deadlines may have been promised to external stakeholders or be driven by calendar dates such as year-end or sharing results with the stock market.

If you cannot change the dates to minimize the amount of work happening at any one time, at least the schedule will highlight the busy times, and unfortunately those peaks in workload have to be managed around. Look for and be aware of when you or the team is likely to be busy – and therefore under stress. Being conscious of those calendar clashes will help you take action to minimize the impact. For example:

- Try to do as much as possible in advance, down to creating empty documents ready to be filled in or having pre-meeting conversations with key stakeholders.

- Decline meetings or reschedule them to avoid the busy period.

- Minimize your other work commitments like professional development activities during that time.

- Recruit extra help to see you through the busy period.

- Block out time in your calendar so you can focus on your projects during that time.

- Make your colleagues aware so they can plan too.

- Plan your personal time to be as low stress as possible, for example organizing a meal plan and getting the support you need for caring responsibilities if possible.

- Plan something fun for the team to do after you've all got through a busy time.

Remember, if you change dates on your combined schedule as a result of identifying busy times or staff absence, make sure those changes flow through to any individual project plans.

> I think the hardest part [of managing multiple projects] was to manage important milestones that were planned to happen at the same time and required full attention over a period of time. That would give very long work hours and it was not always possible to plan my way out of it. I learned that a maximum of two projects at a time was optimal to make sure I delivered the quality I wanted. Now that I am working in agile, this has changed, so we still have many activities in parallel that would previously have been defined as different projects, but now it's all in the same backlog and I can prioritize. This is really great because it helps avoid those conflicts between parallel running projects with different priorities.
>
> Dorte Frejwald, product owner, pharma industry

Rolling wave planning

Rolling wave planning, also known as progressive elaboration, is a technique to use when it's difficult (or pointless) to plan too far ahead. The APM Planning, Monitoring and Control Specific Interest Group *Planning, Scheduling, Monitoring and Control Guide* (2015) defines rolling wave planning as 'the planning density that is achieved at different moments in time. Primarily more detailed planning in the immediate future and less detailed planning towards the end of the project.'

Rolling wave planning gives you the ability to plan in smaller, incremental, steps. Smaller steps are easier to track and manage, and they take less time to schedule because you are only planning in detail for work that is on the short-term horizon.

The schedule is made up of waves: each wave has tasks planned at an appropriate level of detail, or density. Use high density, detailed planning for the tasks on the short-term horizon. This could represent the next month or 90 days or any other time period that makes sense for the overall duration of the project. This represents a full, in-depth schedule of the work that needs to happen during that period.

The next wave – the medium-term horizon – is made up of tasks planned at medium density: the tasks will have a longer duration and be less granular but they still represent the effort involved.

Finally, the long-term horizon is represented in one or more waves where tasks represent large clusters of work or phases. The tasks are not granular but act more as place markers for activities that are yet to be fully thought though and scheduled.

As the team undergoes the work, the project manager can constantly review the schedule and add more detail to the next waves as this is known. Consequently, you end up with a plan that is frequently revisited, refined and elaborated in a timely way.

Benefits of rolling wave planning

On many projects, you won't know exactly what the work is going to look like later on. Some projects have evolving scope or high levels of complexity, where you don't really know what's going to be required as you move through the work.

The exact project tasks required might depend on the outcome of the design phase or may change once you've carried out customer focus groups, for example. Maybe you have agreed to roll out a new service to certain customers, and the intention is to deploy it to everyone if it's a success. Your sponsor expects to see the timeline for the whole effort, but the exact deployment timetable is going to depend on the order you extend the service to customers, and you don't know that yet.

If you cannot predict what's coming with any degree of certainty, there's not a lot of point in creating a detailed project schedule. You will only have to change it again later and you may have inadvertently set expectations with stakeholders that you then need to revisit. Rolling wave planning reduces the amount of planning upfront. Managers like that because it means they feel the team can get started on delivery work and they start seeing progress more quickly.

I used rolling wave planning on a project to implement organizational changes to comply with new legislation, the full details of which had not yet been released by the regulator. Guidance notes and details were coming out week by week. That shaped the prioritization of project work and changed how we wanted to respond. The schedule evolved iteratively over time as new information was known.

Rolling wave planning is not the lazy way to get around the effort of scheduling. It's a calculated move to show progress with creating a realistic and reasonable schedule, which makes it a good technique to use when you have multiple projects, because you are often under pressure to get going with delivery right now.

How to create a rolling wave plan

A rolling wave plan starts with knowing the major milestones or governance points. These become your wave points: the boundaries of each wave of planning. These could be anchored by project phases, major deliverables, key governance review points or simply that you have chosen to plan in three-month increments.

Next, create a project schedule for the first wave, in conjunction with the team. Look at the tasks that need to be completed in that timeframe and plan them out in detail. Then review the next wave. As you won't have all the information for bottom-up, detailed planning, think about the work you have to complete from the top down. Include larger, longer tasks that represent groups of activity.

If there is a task that runs into the next wave, for example an activity which crosses the wave point, then plan that to the level of detail relevant to where the task starts. There is no point in cutting the task halfway through or changing the dates of your governance boundaries to fit. Plan flexibly: don't stop scheduling tasks halfway through their duration just because they happen to cross a milestone.

Finally, include the long-range tasks. These are tasks towards the later parts and end of your project that can be scheduled at a low density. Include buckets of activity, phases and generic tasks that serve to represent what will be planned in detail once you get nearer.

The end result is a plan with different levels of task density scheduled in waves. An example of what the chart will look like is shown in Figure 4.4. Don't forget that as time moves on you will need to revise those swathes of medium- and low-density activity with more granular planning. It's good practice to book out time to spend elaborating the next iteration of the plan as you get closer to the relevant timeframe because people's calendars get booked up. As you will need input from the project team, you can book planning meetings or workshops now to use for creating the next iteration of the schedule. The planning work for a project using progressive elaboration never stops.

FIGURE 4.4   Rolling wave planning

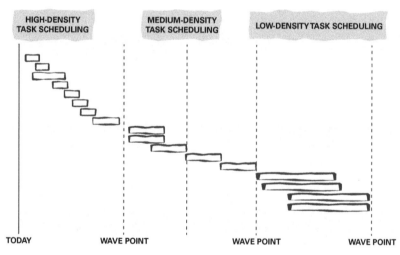

As you create a rolling wave plan, engage stakeholders in what you are doing and explain what the plan represents. In particular, make sure they are aware that, as you have not yet planned in detail, it is difficult (if not impossible) to guarantee an end date for the project. Stakeholders need to be aware that as you schedule in greater detail, tasks may push any anticipated project closure date forward or backward. If the delivery date is fixed, that may mean they have to make decisions about what scope can be realistically achieved in the time.

In a multi-project environment, priorities change quickly. Rolling wave planning for your project cuts out the effort of detailed planning where it's difficult to do so. If priorities then change, you haven't spent a lot of time creating a detailed schedule for a project that is no longer top priority. In addition, the team can plan quite far ahead because the schedule has less detail in the low-density waves, and that can help you review the impact of projects on each other. You can use the medium- and low-density tasks to inform your overall consolidated schedule and to look for overlaps and dependencies between projects.

Use rolling wave planning where it makes sense to do so. It can feel like a time-saving technique but it is not a real shortcut, because you do still have to do the planning; it is simply happening at a different point.

Task-level planning

The big picture plan and a consolidated view of what's happening when are helpful tools, but you still also have to juggle all the individual tasks. There are four tactics that help particularly well for multi-project planning and scheduling at a task level: identifying immovable tasks; identifying tasks with wiggle room; using a standard weekly report; and using an action log.

Identify immovable tasks

Look across your schedules for tasks that cannot move. The dates might be fixed because they have been promised to a customer, or they are on the critical path of your project, or for another reason. Status update meetings where you have to show deliverables to a client, approval dates and sign off dates are typically events that don't move. Meeting-driven dates like fixed governance meetings, project boards, quarterly review boards, committees and so on are also normally planned far in advance and unlikely to move.

You will most likely have items to prepare in advance of these fixed points, for example a demo, meeting papers, presentations or reports. Prioritize meeting the requirements for those immovable tasks. If you're having difficulty knowing what tasks to prioritize on a daily basis, the activities that cannot move are going to be where to focus your effort.

> I work in a small e-commerce website development agency. I manage multiple projects but in my current view, each client is a 'project' with multiple tasks and projects going on. I help manage four large clients and three additional 'occasional' clients. Our entire team is remote. For me to get everything done and work not to fall into the cracks, it takes a good project management tool which provides notices on past due projects; a notebook for to-do lists, ideas etc. (thankfully also built into the tool); agendas for internal and client calls which I add to throughout the week. It requires almost daily planning/scheduling as new requests come in daily and range in size and priority. This is probably one of the biggest challenges.
>
> I am comfortable working with the stakeholders and thankfully most do not require more than a bi-weekly call to discuss ongoing and new projects. However, some clients have access to a Slack channel which they use to pop in, ask questions and discuss new work. So this means while there's not an abundance of business calls there is a LOT of communication. Some clients prefer email, which is my least favourite form of communication for receiving new requests. And still yet some clients have access to their own client board to assign tasks on ClickUp. Abundance of communication styles with multiple clients. Everyone is different and it would be ideal but impossible to consolidate that.
>
> Megan, project manager, USA

Identify tasks with wiggle room

The opposite of tasks that have fixed dates is tasks that have wiggle room: there is some flexibility in their scheduling. Identifying the tasks with the most slack helps you deal with emergencies and last-minute problems on other projects because you can use that flexibility to your advantage.

Let's say you have a task on your list of things to work on this week, and you know the dates allow for some room for manoeuvre. You want to get it done, but it doesn't absolutely have to be done for a couple more weeks. An issue pops up, either on this project or a different project. Because you know there is wiggle room in your schedule for this task, you can push it out to next week and deal instead with whatever crisis is pulling your attention. You don't get stressed about having to reschedule what you planned to do because you know it isn't going to negatively affect your overall ability to complete the work on time.

Eventually, a task with wiggle room becomes a task with a fixed date: it needs to be done at some point, and if you keep delaying it and delaying it, ultimately you are going to arrive at the deadline. However, until that happens, you have some flexibility. Identify where the flexibility exists so you can use it to your advantage if you need it.

Use a standard weekly report

Research into the behaviours of over 2,300 people by Erica and Mike Schultz of the RAIN Group (Schultz and Schultz, 2021) shows that 44 per cent of extremely productive people track progress weekly, compared to 13 per cent of everyone else. If you want to feel more productive, a weekly report is a good tactic.

A simple standard weekly report summarizes what was achieved this week and what will be achieved next week. It is useful for task-level planning because it's a way of holding yourself accountable for the major project activities that you planned to achieve this week. Anything that did not get achieved this week is carried forward to next week's report.

I open up last week's report on a Monday to identify what I said would be the priority tasks for the coming week. Those activities become my focus for the week, so that when I report on a Friday what I've achieved, I can say that these tasks are completed. The report goes to my manager and major project stakeholders on a Friday afternoon, in the form of a colour-coded email – in my experience, opening an attachment is too much work for some people, so the report text appears in the body of the email itself. Tasks that are complete are coloured green, tasks that are delayed but not by much are coloured orange, and tasks that weren't started at all or couldn't start are coloured red.

The RAG colour coding scheme is commonly used by project professionals and you may be familiar with it already. RAG stands for Red, Amber, Green, the colours of traffic lights. Organizations set the threshold for what each colour means. For example, Red could mean that a task will not hit the published completion date and/or is more than 30 per cent overspent. If your organization does not have definitions for the colours, it's OK to use your own professional judgement. Typically, Red means management attention is required as a task is stuck and the project team can't unblock it alone, Amber means the task has gone awry but the team has a plan to address the situation, and Green means the work is on track. Some organizations also use Blue to mean 'completed', making the acronym BRAG.

Save time on Friday by having the report open on your computer for most of the week. As you complete something, update the report. As new tasks appear that need to be added to the priority list for next week, write them on. Copy and paste this week's report to create the foundations of next week's. There is a status report template to use as a starting point in Chapter 5 and an alternative version in Appendix 2.

> Managing multiple projects is difficult, as soon as you feel like one project is on track and understood, something else goes off the rails on another project. I like to manage my own tasks from one consolidated list, and add in prompts to check in with key team members when I delegate something to them, to ensure everything stays on track. Writing things down and not relying on memory are key. As are structured reports and reporting periods.
>
> Rachel, project manager, New Zealand

Use an action log

The final tactic for task-level planning is to use an action log. An action log is a simple way to record the tasks that drop out of your meetings, emails, calls and conversations. These are To Do list activities that would not necessarily need to go on your integrated schedule or even your individual project schedules.

You can have a multi-project action log, if you want to keep everything on one project log, or you can create an action log per project if you find it easier to manage that way, and if your team members stay the same across several projects.

Action logs can be created in any software, although it's a bonus to be able to easily update and share the records, and filter by task owner or project. For that reason, I use a spreadsheet, but modern task management apps and project management software would also work. Think about how you want to maintain the list as you set it up. I prefer to have the option to share the log with the team, and for that reason, I have a log per project as my teams do not always overlap. I prefer to have responsibility for updating the log myself, although you could delegate responsibility for updating tasks to the individual task owners.

Another benefit of having a single place for your To Do list tasks is that when you meet with someone, you can filter the action log(s) on their name to see what work is outstanding for them. Then use your meeting time to get updates on all their outstanding tasks. Use the downtime before and after a meeting to catch them for updates: the meeting doesn't necessarily need to be about your project. If you are both attending, there will hopefully be a moment for you to ask about project work.

Resource allocation across multiple projects

Resource management is planning, getting and using the resources that you need to do your project efficiently. Often, organizations use 'resources' as an unfriendly shorthand for 'people'. The term can also mean equipment, services, software, hardware, supplies, raw materials and anything else you need in order to make the project go forward efficiently.

When you manage multiple projects, the biggest resource challenge is normally people. You might have to order supplies or book equipment, but that is easier to manage than people's time. In order to make sure you are using individuals' time in the most effective and efficient way, you first need to know who is going to be working on the project with you. These people form part of your project team and are normally subject matter experts or others who can contribute to the work.

Typically, these people will work on your project on a part-time basis. They might be working on several of your projects, or supporting another project manager with their work. Maybe they have 'day job' responsibilities in an operational capacity.

> In our small architecture office the project managers are often battling for the same resources. Even though we plan monthly there would always be shifting needs last minute. We decided to have a weekly project management meeting prior to our weekly staff meeting where we would debate any shifting or new priorities and skillsets of resources to make sure everything could be accommodated, no one was over or underutilized, and everyone was hitting their minimum billable hours.
>
> Gillian Hutchison, Portugal

How to secure resources for your projects

People are busy and have other things to do besides work on your projects. That's why it is important to give team leaders and individuals enough notice for the work required. Get commitment for their time as early as you can so they know the work is coming up for them and they can plan for it.

Use your consolidated schedule to plan forward, identifying what support or skills you might need in four or five months' time if you don't currently have resources booked. If you have secured time from an individual, look across all your projects to see how you can best use it, especially if there are lulls in the upcoming work. They could use their project hours to train a colleague, develop new skills so they can support other areas of the project or get ahead on future tasks.

Capacity planning software allows you to see resource assignments across multiple projects and teams. However, many organizations don't have tools that provide this level of data, or a culture that enables forecasting and planning at a granular level. You may find yourself having to plan people's time commitments with just a spreadsheet and using detective work to talk to team leaders about who is available to work on what at what time. This can be time-consuming in itself.

In some situations – for example where your organization does not yet have a mature approach to managing projects – the onus falls to you to ensure you secure support for your work. There are some things you can do to make it easier to make sure that your team members have enough time to dedicate to the work that you need them to do. That starts with understanding who influences decisions around how individuals spend their time – the gatekeepers.

Build relationships with gatekeepers

Build relationships with gatekeepers – the people who manage the priorities and time for subject matter experts and resources who work on your projects. These gatekeepers could be team leaders or department heads. They are typically the line manager of the person whose time you want for your project.

Ideally, you will have built a relationship before you need to ask for someone from their team to support your project. Your internal network is an important source of support for your project. Work by Ron Burt (2000) shaped subsequent thinking about network diversity and shows that 'better connected people enjoy higher returns'. Building an internal network is beyond the scope of this book, but there are some suggestions for building relationships with colleagues later in the book, and there are plenty of good guides to developing professional networking skills. Try to dedicate some time regularly to improving and deepening your professional relationships with colleagues by making time for them, sharing useful information with them, and being interested in what they are doing.

When you need to ask for support from their team members, start by explaining the role that individual would play on the project so that the gatekeeper understands what that person is being asked to do. If you can, show how the project work links to the strategic objectives of the organization or department. This helps demonstrate the value in the work and elevates the ask from simply a task to a contribution to the organization.

It's really important to keep communication channels open with the line managers of your project team members. Make time for regular check-ins with team leaders. This is one of the primary ways that you will find out about upcoming absence, planned holiday and other times when the individual will be unavailable for project work, if the person themselves doesn't let you know.

Certain project team members and stakeholders are senior enough in the organization that you don't need to talk to their manager about their availability and what else they are working on. Talk to them directly. These are the kind of things that you can ask:

- How much time do you/your team/individual have for my project?
- What is your top priority if it's not my project?
- And how can my project and I support you in doing that?

This question is not an offer to take on more work for their top priority project. It's a way to uncover how you can manage your project work in a way that doesn't interfere with their priority goals. For example, you may be able to work around their other commitments by only scheduling meetings with them on a Tuesday.

- When do you/they have upcoming leave?
- When will you/they be really busy?

As we've seen, getting visibility of absences is helpful for your project planning. Knowing their busy times is useful too. For example, if you're working with the finance department, there will be particular times in the financial year when they are very busy. Try and find out what those are for the people in the project team.

- What roadblocks do you see?
- What's coming up that I don't know about that you think might be a problem?

There could be activities or events happening in the future that you're not aware of. Ask open-ended questions to uncover things that might create problems or opportunities for your project schedules.

Keep everything under review

Whatever you hear from line managers or the resources themselves, assume that things will change in the near future. The information you get today is only good for today – who knows what their priorities will be in three months. It's important to monitor progress against your plan (the fourth personal portfolio management principle) and to do that you need accurate, updated information about what people are doing and how much time they continue to have to work on your projects. Keep talking and reviewing, having the same conversation about availability and upcoming work as a way of reminding people about their commitments and also to reassure yourself that they really will be available when you need them. Make changes to the schedule based on that information to ensure it reflects reality.

Resource management across multiple projects is one of the hardest things to manage. Here are some 'voices from the trenches' from project managers who have experience of trying to secure resources, drawn from a survey for this book:

- Two ICT projects with expectations to utilize same resources. Funding request for additional resources declined. [It was] challenging to meet all delivery requirements – Kirsten

- Biggest challenge was always making stakeholders realize that shared resources among projects without dependencies (not obvious in any one project's plan) are meaningful and require sound cross-functional prioritization – David

- My biggest struggle is that I have multiple projects that often rely on the same resources and stakeholders. Stakeholders want to be seen as 'getting things done' but don't understand the impact on the downline. Project team resources are overextended with both day-to-day operational work and project work. I have seen and experienced this in all four organizations where I have been a project manager. I know I can manage four to eight projects well but not if we keep tapping into the same pool of resources – Lisa

- We have a matrixed team of resources (developers, business analysts, data analysts, quality analysts etc.) that work on our projects and a key success for all of our teams is to turn all project sprints on the same sprint dates (even if one project is just starting and another is finishing, they'll all run three-week sprints with same start and end dates), which allows us to plan resources across projects and have more certainty in the work we can get done with less interruptions and risks – Dana

- I currently have nine active projects of different sizes and the other project manager in my department also has nine, all pulling from the same resource pool and all affecting the same end users. [It] is a nightmare. Throttling the project pipeline and making people wait for the start date of their projects takes strong leadership and people get grumpy but it is vital with shared resources to ensure success – Leah

A lot of the challenges come from the organization around you not being able or willing to understand the logistics and requirements of running multiple projects in parallel. There's no magic bullet for that, but keep communicating and using your documentation and data to demonstrate the impact of resource conflicts on your work.

KEY TAKEAWAYS

- Consolidate and combine project schedules to provide the big picture view across all your projects.

- Identify dependencies between projects to help you schedule and prioritize the work in the right order using a source and target matrix.

- The combined schedule provides better visibility and allows you to identify busy times. It allows you to visualize your commitments and those of your team and make adjustments to ensure neither you nor your colleagues are overloaded.

- Consider rolling wave planning as a way to develop a schedule where you cannot accurately predict the work into the future.

- Identify immovable tasks and tasks with flexible schedules, use weekly reporting and an action log to help with task-level planning.

- Build good relationships with people who supply resources for your project and individual subject matter experts so you can help them commit time to your project.

ACTION STEPS

Your action step from this chapter is to create a consolidated project schedule. Here's how to do it.

- Make sure each of your individual projects has a schedule or timeline.

- Map the dependencies between your projects.

- Choose either the ladder or hot air balloon view to make your consolidated schedule (or decide to try both and see which you prefer).

- Combine your schedules into one overarching timeline.

- Review that schedule to look for resource conflicts and busy times and take appropriate action.

- Start an action log for task-level planning.

References

Amabile, T and Kramer, S (2011) *The Progress Principle*, Harvard Business Review Press, Boston

APM Planning, Monitoring and Control Specific Interest Group (2015) *Planning, Scheduling, Monitoring and Control: The practical project management of time, cost and risk*, APM, Princes Risborough

Bilgin, G, Eken, G, Ozyurt, B, Dikmen, I, Birgonul, M T and Ozorhon, B (2017) Handling project dependencies in portfolio management, *Procedia Computer Science*, 121, 356–63

Burt, R S (2000) The network structure of social capital, *Research in Organizational Behaviour*, 22, 345–423

Clark, D (2021) *The Long Game: How to be a long-term thinker in a short-term world*, Harvard Business Review Press, Boston

Harrin, E (2021) Managing multiple projects: the research, 29 October. Available from https://rebelsguidetopm.com/managing-multiple-projects-the-research (archived at https://perma.cc/73XE-MV4Z)

Horwath, R (2012) The Strategic Thinking Manifesto. Available from www.strategyskills.com/wp-content/uploads/2012/09/The-Strategic-Thinking-Manifesto.pdf (archived at https://perma.cc/WN9L-NMRR)

Schultz, E and Schultz, M (2021) *Not Today: The 9 habits of extreme productivity*, BenBella Books, Dallas

Further reading

Lock, D (2019) *Project Management*, 10th edn, Routledge, Abingdon

Muzio, E (2018) *Iterate: Run a fast, flexible, focused management team*, An Inc. Original, New York

05

Concept #3: People: engaging stakeholders across multiple projects

All projects are done by people, whether you work as part of a large team or are managing and doing the project work by yourself. As well as the people delivering the project, there are other individuals and groups who are affected by the work. Together, these people have the power to influence and shape your projects, and they are the focus of the third concept in the framework, as show in Figure 5.1.

FIGURE 5.1   The People concept in the managing multiple projects framework

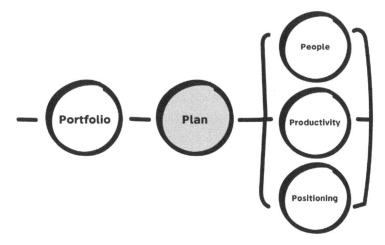

According to a survey by Gallup (2020) employee engagement has a direct correlation to productivity, the delivery of quality outputs, well-being and profitability – all things we want from projects and the people who work on them. However, only 20 per cent of employees are engaged at work (Gallup, 2021). The activities you do to shift someone from being not engaged with your project to engaged can have a huge impact on the perception of project success and the outcomes achieved.

Experienced project managers understand this already. Communication and stakeholder engagement ranks as the second most important skillset for managing multiple projects – second only to planning (Harrin, 2021). However, it isn't easy to engage others. While you might be deeply involved in the project, other people have their own jobs and priorities. While you might have a full understanding of the details of your project, they might not remember why the project is even happening. You may be leading five projects; they may be contributing to several of yours, plus a few being led by someone else, while at the same time being affected by the changes delivered by a couple of others – and of course they have their day jobs too.

The changes, outputs, deliverables and outcomes that your projects are making happen are only part of their world. We need to meet people where they are: as embroiled in multiple aspects of the organization, and contributing and being affected by many of the initiatives that are happening at the same time.

Engaging with people on multiple projects means putting them at the heart of what you are trying to do and understanding what the world looks like from their perspective. Trust me, it looks messy, complicated and busy. Good engagement can make people breathe a sigh of relief as you guide them through what needs to happen.

This chapter is your guide to helping others engage on the projects. You will get new tools for understanding who matters on your projects, which is the starting point for working out how to prioritize your time with the right people. You'll understand the interpersonal skills required to engage with stakeholders across your projects. You'll learn how to set expectations effectively and how to streamline how you interact with others to reduce communications fatigue.

What is stakeholder engagement?

APM (2019) defines stakeholders as 'influential, interested individuals and groups who are affected by projects, programmes or portfolios'. They are the people you work with to deliver the project, whether they have a substantive role to play or are only called upon to do one or two tasks.

In an ideal world, everyone would be fully behind the project and give you their full attention and commitment at all times, regardless of the size of their contribution. However, there are many demands on your colleagues' time, and you aren't the only customer for your suppliers. Stakeholder engagement is the activity that keeps people connected to your projects.

Stakeholders feel involved, heard and valued when they are treated like partners in project delivery instead of simply 'resources' to be booked via a software tool to complete assigned tasks. 'Engagement' is what you do to create those feelings: it is mainly talking, listening, discussion, relationship building, knowledge sharing and targeted interactions designed to increase the likelihood that individuals will participate in the project in the way you want them too.

The purpose of investing time in engagement activities is to increase the chances that people will behave in ways that are conducive to project delivery. In other words, engagement serves to reduce conflict, increase understanding and encourage people to do what you need them to do. In turn, that saves you time chasing up actions and cajoling people who don't work for you into doing their project tasks.

Engagement is twofold: it happens through building positive interest in the work and minimizing negative interest (Harrin, 2020). You are encouraging supportive behaviour and creating an environment where people want to join with you in delivering the projects. At the same time, you are smoothing over resistance to change and influencing those individuals who don't see the point in what you are doing.

There are two things that stakeholders should be engaged in to build positive interest and minimize negative interest:

- The process of managing the projects: how you are doing the work and how you intend to work with them.
- The outcomes of the projects: what you are delivering.

Often stakeholders haven't had as much project experience as you have, especially if you are formally in the role of project manager or spend a lot of your day job working on projects. They need support to be able to operate in a project environment and use the processes you have chosen to get the work done. For example, in a mature project management environment, you will be carrying out risk management, change management, multi-project scheduling, retrospectives or lessons learned and many other things. Stakeholders might not have taken part in any of those formal processes before. They may never have had the need to join a planning workshop or brainstorm a list of requirements and will need support of some kind in order to be able to participate effectively.

In addition to being able to join in with the process, they also need to understand the project's outcomes and what is being created or delivered as a result. That can be broken down further as a sub-set of the project's goals will be their tasks and what role they play on the project, however big or small. Engagement activities help create clarity about their involvement and give them the information and environment required to do their work.

Within those two elements of process and outcomes, being able to engage others starts with understanding what action or behaviour you want to see from them. What do you want the result of the engagement to be? Perhaps it's sharing information with their team, making a decision or taking an action. Once you have clarified your objective, you can then turn your efforts to thinking about how you are going to get that intended result. Engaging others in the work is a core responsibility for anyone managing projects so it is probably something you have some experience doing already. In this book, we will focus on how to switch up the ways you work with others when you are juggling more than one project, so you can win back time in your day.

Working with project sponsors

An individual project might have many stakeholders, but the most important and influential one is normally the project sponsor. This is the person who benefits the most from what the project is delivering or who holds the resources you need to get the work done. Sponsors can be:

- Your direct manager, for example where you are delivering a project for the benefit of your team.
- A senior manager in another department, for example where your project management skills are being used to deliver work that benefits another team or teams.
- A senior manager in the customer organization, for example where your organization is completing work for a client. In this case, you probably have an internal sponsor as well, leading the work on your side.
- Someone else: sponsors can come in lots of different forms!

As someone leading many projects, you will have many project sponsors. Some will be hands-on individuals who take up a lot of your time; others will be happy to let you get on with the work as long as you report progress regularly. According to executives surveyed for the *HBR Project Management Handbook* (Nieto-Rodriguez, 2021), executives spend 32 per cent of their time on projects and the implementation of transformation and change initiatives. That's not very much; it is only around a day and half a week, split between all the projects the person is sponsoring. They may be sponsoring more than one of your projects, or projects for other project managers.

Given that they are busy people with lots of demands on their time (just like you), it's important to think about how best to work with them. If you consider it appropriate, talk to your sponsor about the principle of management by exception. This is a principle of the PRINCE2® project management method that sets agreed boundaries and tolerances for the work. As long as the work is progressing within those boundaries, there is no need for the sponsor to get involved. They will still receive information and formal reporting at the relevant governance points, but you aren't bothering them with small details or copying them in to every email. As soon as the project is expected to go outside of the tolerances set, the project manager alerts the sponsor.

WHAT IS PRINCE2®?

PRINCE2® is a process-based project management method. It stands for Projects IN a Controlled Environment (Version 2). It is a structured and experience-based method, created from the lived experience of thousands of project managers and successful projects and currently overseen by Axelos®, a provider of global best practice. PRINCE2® is a customizable way of managing and controlling project work. It's tailorable and suitable for projects of all sizes, large and small as it is underpinned by principles, themes and processes that are universally applicable.

Tolerances can be set for a number of aspects of the project, at levels that feel comfortable to both the project manager and sponsor. For example:

- Time: the project delivery date can move ± two weeks;
- Cost: the project budget can change ± 10%;
- Quality: the search feature must return results within 0.5 seconds with a tolerance of ± 0.1 second;
- Scope: as long as the mandatory requirements are included, the project team can introduce other requirements as long as time and cost boundaries are respected.

Having these conversations and setting tolerances is very liberating. As long as the project is going to plan and you are confident you are within tolerance, you can get on with the work without needing to constantly provide updates.

As you can imagine, this approach only works when the project sponsor trusts the project manager, and the project manager is empowered to get things done. If you work in an environment where that is possible and reasonable, you can cut some of the overhead of managing up because you only need to get the sponsor involved when things deviate from your agreed plan.

Beyond your relationships with project sponsors, you will also have to work with many other people on your projects. Let's look next at how to make those relationships work effectively.

Managing stakeholders across multiple projects

There are nearly always multiple stakeholders to manage, even on one project. However, the more projects you manage, the more people you have to involve and the greater the number of stakeholders you interact with on a regular basis. That presents some logistical challenges of keeping everyone up-to-date and prioritizing interactions with the people who have the most influence over the end result or project goals. There are two tools that will help you stay on top of the relationships you have with these colleagues: the stakeholder directory and the multi-project stakeholder map.

> Working with different stakeholders/groups is like walking on eggshells while juggling all the balls and singing the alphabet backwards. Check in, don't assume. Communicate the same messages five times and in different ways to get your message across.
>
> Stephene, project manager, Australia

Create a stakeholder directory

Managing multiple projects normally means you are juggling a lot of contacts. You need a way of managing information about them because it can be a lot to hold in your head. A stakeholder directory is a Customer Relationship Management (CRM) system for project people. It can be a spreadsheet, A–Z tabbed notebook or you can use contact management software features in the tools you already have. Use it to record helpful information about your stakeholders.

The basic data points to include are:

- Name;
- Job title;
- Location and time zone if different to yours;
- Telephone number(s);
- Email address;
- Preferred method of communication, for example collaboration tool, via phone or something else;
- What project(s) they are involved in;
- Role on the project(s).

Additional data to include could cover:

- Their past roles in the organization or where they used to work;
- Specialist skills;
- Contact details for their executive assistant if they have one;
- Places they studied or certifications they hold;
- Some personal details, for example hobbies, pets or family members if they have shared this information with you.

So much of building relationships with people is about informal conversations and taking an interest in their work and their life. If they mentioned that they have school-age children, for example, you might bring that up in conversation around the time of the school holidays: 'Are you taking time away from work for the school holidays?' If you find you have something in common, for example you both have cats, you can share a story of what your cat did at the weekend and ask after their pet. These informal chats make use of your interpersonal skills to help build trust and present you as personable, friendly and approachable. You don't need to be best friends with your work colleagues, but being interested in others will help to position you as someone they can go to with questions – or information they think you will find useful. Those small nuggets of information shared in informal chats could help you lead the project more effectively and over time create a concrete network within your organization.

Remember, if you are storing personal data about colleagues, suppliers and other stakeholders, make sure you do so in a secure way, in line with your organization's policies about information protection. Check with the organization's information security team so you comply with current regulation, policy and best practice, and hold yourself personally accountable for how that information is used.

It sounds calculated and manufactured to write out how to engineer interactions in this way with the goal of building relationships with people at work. If you have a great memory for this kind of detail, then you can rely on that. If you are working with many stakeholders in many different settings, then notes can help. They prompt your recall about your last conversations and allow you to create moments for small talk.

Small talk – those quick questions and normally superficial interactions that help pass the time – is actually crucial to building trusted relationships. It's even more important in virtual teams, where it is hard to find a replacement for water-cooler or coffee machine chat. Instead of bumping into someone in the corridor, you have to orchestrate moments for the exchange of pleasantries. For example:

- Send them a link to something you've read that they might enjoy.
- Send something through the post, like a thank you card or handwritten note appreciating their efforts on the project.
- Use time in project team meetings for informal catch-ups and check-ins instead of cramming every moment with project business.
- Seek their opinion on something.

Informal chat gives other people the opportunity to ask you questions as well and you are building ongoing relationships, without it feeling like you are hassling them for status updates.

In a diverse workplace, you may find that your working styles do not align to those of your colleagues. Consider how you can make adjustments to accommodate the needs of stakeholders. For example, turning on captioning for videos shown in meetings, providing presentation materials in advance, choosing an accessible venue, requesting attendees do not wear strong scents, allowing people to stand and move around the room if that is more comfortable for them and so on.

Create a multi-project stakeholder map

Once you've got a directory of people you work with, it's time to see how those relationships overlap in your project ecosystem. Creating a multi-project stakeholder map will highlight where individuals or groups have a role in more than one of your projects. To do that, list all the people you work with and group them by project. You can create this as a mindmap or a list in a document or spreadsheet, whichever works best for you. Link people to the projects they are interested in.

> The most difficult situations to deal with are always related to the people on the project; difficult personalities, stakeholders that bring corporate politics into the mix, team members that are very protective of the information that the project needs to move forward. I've learned over the years to really work to identify the key contacts for each project and OVER communicate with the teams. So many issues/ challenges I've run into with projects I've managed have been because of mismatched expectations, missing communications, not including the right people at the beginning of the project, and identifying stakeholders that have sway in the project, too late.
>
> Steph Holmes

Next, look for sources of conflict or opportunity, especially where stakeholders have influence over several projects. Sources of conflict include:

- Time: where one stakeholder is pivotal to so many projects, they will not have time to serve each effectively.

- Expectations: where stakeholders have different views about what one or more projects will deliver, for example where a stakeholder on one project is pushing for a deliverable that will negatively impact a stakeholder on another project.

- Resources: where you don't have enough stakeholders to fulfil the resource requirements of one or more projects, perhaps because a team manager has assumed someone can meet the needs of multiple projects and now you've done the planning you can see that isn't going to be feasible.

- Leadership: where one project or group of related projects has more than one person in a leadership or sponsorship role.

If you identify potential points of conflict, take steps to have conversations with the relevant stakeholders. Explain what you've noticed and suggest ways to address that. You may need to bring several stakeholders together – even if they technically operate on different projects – in order to facilitate an outcome that everyone is satisfied with. In particular, setting realistic expectations is important to ensure everyone has clarity and can agree about what is to come.

You can uncover sources of conflict through active listening, interviews, conversations, observation and using what you know about office politics and the culture of your working environment. You may not have all the information at the time you start thinking about stakeholders in this way, so be prepared to revisit and revise your notes as you learn more about how individuals and projects interrelate.

It is worth acting on potential conflict even before it becomes a 'real' problem. Heading off problems saves time later and creates a more pleasant working environment for everyone. It's easier to discuss issues before they have happened as people are less emotionally invested in the outcome before it is personally affecting them or their team. Sources of opportunity include:

- Resources: creating pools of subject matter experts who could advise and support across projects.

- Communication: merging communications to stakeholders who share common interests across several projects (there is more on this later in the chapter).

- Task consolidation: team members performing the same task on several projects could find it advantageous to consolidate their work.

Act on these potential opportunities too. Talk to the individuals you have identified about how work could be combined or streamlined as a result of their involvement in several of the projects you are leading.

FIGURE 5.2   Example of a multi-project stakeholder mindmap

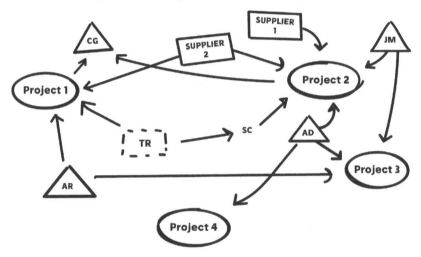

Figure 5.2 shows an example of a multi-project stakeholder mind-map for one project manager, using team member initials. You can see that there are several people involved in multiple projects either because of their subject matter expertise or because they are in a leadership position. Key contacts are marked with squares. The connections help you visualize an individual stakeholder's project ecosystem. That context provides insightful information into how you can engage with them. It shows you:

- What they are involved with

  o Use this information to discuss their project priorities with them: which one is most important to them?

- ○ Does that align with the importance given by other stakeholders to the work?
- What they will talk about when you meet them
  - ○ Use this information to plan for your conversations
  - ○ What else might they be interested in?

The multi-project stakeholder map is simple to create and a powerful tool for understanding exactly who you need to work with on a day-to-day basis.

How to prioritize time with stakeholders

Between your project sponsors and other key contacts, your stakeholder directory is probably looking quite busy. How can you find time to plan to engage all these people and then carry out those engagement activities? It might feel like you won't have time to do anything else.

In an ideal world, we would have all the time necessary to build deep, trusted working relationships with people across all our projects. In the real world, there simply aren't enough hours in the day to do that. That's why you should prioritize stakeholders so you can invest your limited time on the relationships that matter most.

Stakeholder saliency is a model created by Mitchell et al (1997) with the goal of providing a framework for explaining 'to whom and to what managers actually pay attention'. They define salience as 'the degree to which managers give priority to competing stakeholder claims', which makes it a great tool to use for managing multiple groups of stakeholders.

The theory of stakeholder salience shows who really counts on the project. And when you know that, you can better prioritize your time. The model combines the attributes of legitimacy, urgency and power to establish stakeholders' relative importance and influence.

Legitimacy is a measure of how valid their views are; how much of a right a stakeholder has to make requests of the project. For example, they could have a contractual right to make demands of the project, or a legitimate business interest – perhaps they are going to use the software you are building.

Power is a measure of how much influence they have over the actions and outcomes of the project. That influence can come from a variety of sources such as:

- Hierarchical status in the organization or project team, for example being the project sponsor or chief executive.
- Prestige or soft power, for example being a respected and trusted subject matter expert in a relevant domain.
- Ownership of resources, for example being the budget holder or line manager for the people doing the work.

Urgency refers to how much attention they demand and how quickly they expect their requests to be dealt with. Typically, the more important someone considers themselves to be, the more unacceptable it is to them to face any delay in response. Their request could be genuinely time-sensitive, but it is equally possible that it is not.

The three attributes combined give you useful information about how someone may interact with the projects. It shows how they could wield their influence. Someone who appears on your stakeholder map as part of several projects could hold more influence than someone who appears only once, but that's not always the case. The purpose of using the saliency model is to uncover more about how stakeholders will engage with you and where to spend your limited time. The more attributes a project stakeholder has, the more it is worth prioritizing your time with them.

How to use the saliency model

Add information about saliency to your stakeholder directory. Table 5.1 shows one way to do this. For each person's involvement with each project, note your assessment of the attributes. Remember that some stakeholders may appear in more than one project, but with different levels of influence on each. Consider:

- Do they hold a position of power over the project?
- Do they have a legitimate claim over the work of the project?
- Is there something that is making their requests very urgent at the moment?

There are eight combinations of power, legitimacy and urgency that create eight categories of stakeholder. Mitchell et al define these groups as follows.

Definitive stakeholders: These stakeholders tick all the boxes. They hold power in the project setting, they have a legitimate claim over the work being done and they can use urgency to shape what gets acted on. They might not wield their influence in all ways at all times, but they could if they wanted to. An example would be your project sponsor.

Dominant stakeholders: These stakeholders have the attributes of power and legitimacy. They are probably recognized by your organization in some way, such as holding a position of hierarchical power or sitting on a committee or board. These are the kinds of stakeholders who expect (and receive) formal reports and briefings. An example would be your project governance board.

Dangerous stakeholders: You may not have stakeholders who fit into this category, demonstrating the attributes of power and urgency but with no legitimate claim over the project. As they don't have a legitimate claim to the work being done, they may use their power to influence in destructive ways as they try to 'muscle in' on the project. An example would be someone using coercive power to try to influence outcomes, for example threatening to have you removed from the project if you do not take a particular action.

Dependent stakeholders: These stakeholders have the attributes of legitimacy and urgency but do not have any real power on the project. An example would be local residents in the town where your team is building a new facility on the edge of a nature reserve. They are unable to directly affect the outcomes but they have a legitimate interest in how the land is used and their involvement will be time-sensitive. They depend on the actions of others – stakeholders with power – to effect change.

TABLE 5.1   Example saliency information to include in a stakeholder directory

Name	Role	Project	Power	Legitimacy	Urgency	Category	Potential action
Person A	Tech team lead	Project 1	Y	Y	Y	Definitive	Engage fully
Person B	Marketing rep	Project 1	Y	Y	N	Dominant	Engage fully in anticipation of urgency
Person C	Customer rep	Project 1	Y	N	Y	Dangerous	No legitimate authority on the project but could use their power in inappropriate ways – engage, plan to mitigate impact of their actions
Person D	Sponsor	Project 2	N	Y	Y	Dependent	May need to align with a stakeholder with power to affect change – engage, plan to respond to their actions
Person E	Team lead	Project 1	Y	N	N	Dormant	Watching brief
Person F	Governance expert	Project 2	N	Y	N	Discretionary	Watching brief
Person E	Sponsor	Project 1	N	N	Y	Demanding	Watching brief
Person A	Tech team lead	Project 2	N	N	N	Not a stakeholder	Not necessary to engage at this time

Dormant stakeholders: These stakeholders have power but they aren't using it as they don't have any particular reason to engage with the project at this time.

Discretionary stakeholders: This group represents people with a legitimate interest in the work but no power or influence to shape the direction of the work. These stakeholders are often on the receiving end of corporate philanthropy, so if one of your projects decommissions old staff laptops and reformats them so they can be donated to and used by local schools, the schools become discretionary stakeholders.

Demanding stakeholders: These stakeholders have concerns they consider to be urgent, but no power and no true legitimate claim to participate in the project. Mitchell et al describe them as 'mosquitoes buzzing in the ears of managers' and give the example of a single protestor holding a placard outside an organization.

Non-stakeholders: Finally, your analysis may identify people who are not stakeholders at this time because they have none of the attributes in the saliency model. However, think carefully before putting people in this group, especially if they have sought you out and are acting as if they are stakeholders. Do you really have the full picture? Why do they think they should be involved in the work in some capacity? An ignored stakeholder can quickly become a time-consuming problem for a project so be cautious about dismissing individuals or groups as irrelevant to the work.

As someone managing multiple projects, you need to be smart about where to spend your time. The more attributes someone has, the more likely it is that they need to be on your radar for stakeholder engagement. However, stakeholders don't stay in fixed categories. Their influence over the project (and each other) changes with time. For example, a dominant stakeholder can become definitive when they want to get something done. That adds a degree of urgency due to their expected deadline and they gain the urgency attribute as a result. Power, authority, urgency, legitimacy and influence can be lost or gained, slowly over time or in an instant. Stay tuned in to how stakeholders are shifting on your projects.

My colleague resigned and I was left his complex projects. As a junior project manager, I was used to managing the small projects with not as much engagement required. Taking on more complex projects has made me realise more stakeholder engagement is required to update on progress, planning before a change window is arranged and making sure everyone is on the same page. Communication for me has been key. Taking 10 to 15 minutes before jumping into my day to analyse what needs to be done on a project has worked for me, to organize my thoughts and day ahead. Every day I am learning something new and I am mindful to keep my lessons learned in my toolbox for when I need it.

Jenny Harrison, telecommunications project manager, South Africa

The saliency model, and the analysis created for your projects, will give you a picture of which stakeholders are most influential on any given project. Once you have the list, look over your analysis to spot overlaps between projects. Review the list and pick out the stakeholders who need most of your attention at this time (remember: stakeholders can move between categories so your analysis is only relevant at this moment). The attention that stakeholders command depends on both how relevant they are to the project, as identified by your analysis, and how much time you have to work with them. Assuming you have the time, the actions for engaging stakeholders for each of the categories where they demonstrate more than one attribute are:

- Definitive: fully engage this group;
- Dominant: fully engage this group: they are likely to have requests with deadlines at some point so it's important to stay connected to their expectations;
- Dangerous: engage with a view to mitigating the impact of their potential actions (hopefully, you don't have too many of these);
- Dependent: engage with a view to understanding their perspective. If they receive power, through virtue of influencing a powerful stakeholder or moving into a position of power themselves, you will need a plan to respond to their concerns.

Anyone who falls outside these categories should stay on your radar, but with a watching brief: there's no need to take specific, targeted action at this time. Include them in communications and meetings where relevant but focus your energy on the people who matter more to project success at this time.

If saliency theory doesn't work for you, think of other ways you can identify priority stakeholders across all your projects. The interest and influence matrix is a popular tool used on single projects and is a simpler approach for stakeholder analysis, plus you may already be familiar with that (if not, it's covered in another of my books, *Engaging Stakeholders on Projects*, 2020). However, the tool or approach used to do this doesn't matter: your goal is to review the community of stakeholders you work with regularly to identify the relationships that matter most. That's where you need to spend your limited time.

Create a drop-everything list

As we've seen, not all stakeholders command equal attention, especially when your attention is necessarily limited by working with a large network of contacts across multiple projects. That's why it is important to think about whom you allow to pull your focus.

A 'drop everything list' is a list of the key stakeholders for whom you will drop everything to take their call. It's the people who really matter to you and your work. If you are stressed or stretched for time, these are the people who take priority. Anyone else can wait.

Your list is made up of key work contacts like executive stakeholders and the project sponsors of your biggest or most important projects as well as people from your family life, for example childcare providers or the carer for an elderly relative. You could mark the contacts on your phone with an abbreviation or special ring tone, or flag them in your email system or collaboration tools as VIPs where that's possible. But you don't need to write the list down or call out those contacts in any way – the thought process of considering those contacts and having them in your head is enough. If your list is more people than you can comfortably hold in your head, you probably need to re-think who your priority contacts really are.

Setting stakeholder expectations

It takes time to deal with miscommunication and people who don't complete their tasks. You don't have a lot of time when you have a personal portfolio of projects to look after, so it helps to set expectations effectively. When everyone has realistic expectations of what they have to do or what they can expect, you save time later because you shouldn't have to follow up or repeat yourself so often.

Being seen as someone who helps others understand their role and responsibilities and provides clarity on the tasks ahead can also help you position yourself as someone who is easy to work with. Being perceived as someone stakeholders know, like and trust is another factor for building solid working relationships which in turn contribute to people making the time to do the work that's expected of them for your project.

There are three different types of expectations to manage:

- Expectations of someone doing project work;
- Expectations of someone receiving project work;
- Your own expectations.

Setting expectations for someone doing project work

Unless it's just you working on the project, you will have to ask people to do tasks. The clearer you can make your task, the easier it is for them to understand what you need them to do. People don't have the time or the inclination to work it out themselves because everyone has competing priorities. If it is easy to work with you, your work goes to the top of their list: another reason why honing those interpersonal skills is important. Typically, you'll want to explain:

- What the task is;
- Why it is important;
- When it needs to be done by;
- Any quality standards, processes or protocols they need to follow or abide by;
- Anything else that is important for them to know.

Before you start the conversation, check over your stakeholder map and see if they are likely to be involved in any of your other projects. If they are, use your discussion to talk about all the upcoming tasks you need their help with.

Good communication skills help you craft a message that makes it easy for the recipient to understand what you want from them. Making a really clear ask starts with knowing what it is that we want the person to do (in this case, get on the phone). The task needs to be relevant to them and make it clear that you think it is their job to do the task.

Here's a formula for asking someone to get involved in your project.

- *This project will* + short description of what the project is going to do, for example change a process, make a product, update a system, add new features, onboard a new client.
- *It's an opportunity to* + benefit statement, for example sell more, save time, increase customer satisfaction, decrease complaints and so on.
- *Your expertise will* + explain what you need them to do, for example help us craft really good user requirements, smooth the way with the regulator, be important to secure the backing of a big client, enable us to build the best solution or similar.
- *I understand from* + name of someone important to them or influential *that this is your area.*
- *Who would be the right person from your team to work with us on this?*

I tend to ask the 'who would be the right person from your team?' question even if I know the person is the only individual on the team with the right skills or doesn't have any direct reports. It is a less direct way of asking them to commit to the project, and people tend to accept that the only correct person to support the project is them, which results in them volunteering their services.

If you are asking someone for a smaller, one-off piece of work that doesn't require them to join a project team, change how you phrase the ask to be relevant in that situation. For example:

> I'm working on a project that will make it easier for customers to find and agree to our terms and conditions. We're trying to reduce the number of customer complaints and free up the service team to do other work, like supporting that project your boss kicked off last month. We could really do with the support of someone in the legal team to review the updated document, which will be ready by the end of the month. Would you be the right person to take that on, if I could get it to you in the first few days of next month?

You are clearly setting out what you need (the document reviewed) and when you would prefer the work to happen (from the first few days of next month). From there, you can negotiate whether they are the right person and how long they need to complete the task. Once you've gained agreement, put that in writing to them or log it somewhere on your shared task management software so they have a record of what they've committed to (or been committed to by their manager).

You might also want to set some expectations about how you are going to work together. For example, how are you going to communicate with each other? What channels are you going to use? How are you going to get in touch with people, if it's an emergency? What are the expectations for a response?

Time is the biggest challenge for setting expectations with a colleague regarding project work. Typically, you are working with subject matter experts who have the skills and knowledge to know what to do. They just don't have the time to get to your work given their other priorities. You can address this upfront if you think it might be an issue for your project. Explain that you know they have other commitments. Ask how they see your project fitting into their overall workload and what priority it has.

Remember, someone has to work on the low priority projects. While it would be great to believe all our work is top priority, ultimately, it probably isn't. For example, I ran a requirements workshop in a hospital when one of the key stakeholders – a senior nurse – was called away to see a patient. Treating patients was more important than attending a meeting about an IT project (of course), even though for me, getting that meeting done was top priority because without agreement on the requirements we couldn't move the project on.

Anyone who has an operational job is more likely to prioritize that work because it keeps the organization running. There's no point doing a change project that launches in six months if your business has collapsed in the meantime as no one is answering the phones. Be realistic about what priority your projects really have when viewed through the eyes of others.

Setting expectations for someone receiving project work

Your project sponsors and key stakeholders also have expectations that need to be managed. They are normally interested in things like:

- How long will the work take?
- When can I have it/use it/see it?
- What am I getting for my money?
- How much has been spent already?
- Is it the quality I expected?
- Does it meet my needs and requirements?

The best way to manage expectations is to be open and honest about what can be realistically achieved with the time and budget available. You will likely be challenged about that and asked to deliver more for less. Present options: everything is possible with the right amount of time, budget and resources. The balance of how much to invest for the desired outcome is ultimately their choice.

Have an explicit conversation about when they can expect things to be delivered, and tell them about the other projects you are working on. They need to know that you are not 100 per cent dedicated to this piece of work, and neither is the team. If they want to lobby your other project sponsors behind the scenes to get their work moved up the priority list, then they can, but for now it sits within your work portfolio and you will work on it for the amount of scheduled time available.

When problems occur, as they most likely will, explain the impact of those on the dates and budget that have already been agreed. Your project portfolio and any resource planning information will be helpful tools to show what is achievable with the commitments the team already has.

Try to uncover the way your stakeholders prefer to receive information. Someone who needs all the facts will respond better to a detailed data-driven analysis that leads to a logical conclusion. Someone who is a big picture thinker might need a diagram that explains options. If you are presenting to a project board, you'll need to create a briefing that supports a number of preferences.

Cautious optimism in these discussions is OK; promising the moon on a stick because you feel backed into a corner is not. Ask for more time to assess the impact or promise to give them estimates by the end of the day (or a time period that feels realistic to you) if you feel under pressure to commit to something on the spot. Then take the time to reflect and discuss with the experts on the team so you can present something realistic.

Setting your own expectations

Finally, think about how realistic your own expectations are. You are juggling several pieces of work, plus potentially a day job as well. That's a lot already. You probably have a maximum of five or six hours of productive work in you, per day. A good rule of thumb is to 'book' yourself to work at 80 per cent capacity. In other words, leave a 20 per cent buffer in the week so you have time to deal with emergencies, attend team meetings, take lunch breaks and address those ad hoc things that you can't avoid. That could look like keeping one day a week clear of meetings, or ring-fencing some time each day.

You don't have to physically block the time in your calendar at all: use the 80 per cent capacity rule as a mental reminder not to max out your week. There's more on personal time management in Chapter 6.

Streamlining project communications

As we've seen, a lot of stakeholder engagement is communication. It's the fifth principle of personal portfolio management: communicating project status and providing recommendations for actions to your manager, project sponsors and other key stakeholders. Communication goes wider than simply providing status updates and proposals for action because a lot of modern knowledge work is communication. Think of all the emails and instant messages you get in a day. Think of all the staff briefings and phone calls. It is not surprising that stakeholders suffer from communication fatigue. There is just so much, it's hard to pay attention to it all.

Streamlining project communications means looking at where you can combine messages and meetings. There are two benefits to this:

· It makes communications easier to deliver because there is less for you to do.
· It helps stakeholders avoid communication fatigue.

Trust me, they will thank you!

Below, we'll look at five ways you can streamline project communications to make them faster, easier and more relevant to the people who matter. The five ways to do this are:

· Combining meetings;
· Streamlining reporting;
· Creating countdown plans;
· Creating communications calendars;
· Recording decisions.

Combining project meetings

Projects involve a lot of meetings. For example, project managers attend Project Management Office or departmental meetings that involve giving updates on and talking about several projects. There is also the opportunity to talk about multiple projects in stakeholder and team meetings, even though my research for this book shows that the default position for 28 per cent of project managers is to keep a meeting focused on one particular project, as shown in Figure 5.3.

FIGURE 5.3   Per cent of project managers responding to the question: Do you have meetings with stakeholders where more than one project is discussed?

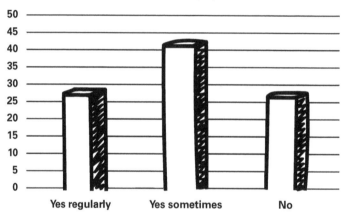

Consider how you can combine project updates from several projects into one meeting. Instead of having multiple conversations with the same stakeholder throughout the week, can you combine everything you want to talk to them about across all of your projects, and just have one session? Book a time with them, create an agenda that covers all the projects they're involved with, and be prepared for any conversations that may come up as a result.

Once, I worked with a sponsor who was sponsoring two of my projects. I arranged a meeting to discuss one of the projects and prepared in detail to cover that. The agenda was focused purely on that one project which was the topic for discussion. However, he kept asking about the other project too. I had not prepared to provide status updates and data related to the other project, but I did my best. As I stumbled through the briefing, explaining what I could remember, I learned a hard lesson: just because we compartmentalize projects, doesn't mean that stakeholders do the same. For him, the meeting was just an opportunity to meet 'his' project manager and catch up on all the work he was interested in.

The agenda can list out the projects in order of priority, with sub-topics for the key things that need to be covered in the meeting. In my experience, executives who are sponsoring or tangentially involved with several projects have a lot on, and sometimes benefit from a quick recap of what the project is and the current status before you get into the specifics, especially if they are not part of the core team.

However, something I have found when dealing with very busy stakeholders, especially senior stakeholders, is that they don't have a lot of time. Be prepared to jump to the essentials in the meeting. Make sure that you know what it is that you want to get out of your time with that individual. If your time is cut, dive straight into that part of the conversation, whether it's making decisions or getting them to take action or asking them to approve something. Those action-orientated outcomes are more valuable than providing a generic progress update because they can read that for themselves in a written report. Use their time wisely because you won't get very much of it.

Another option to consider is running multi-project lessons learned meetings and multi-project closure meetings where it is appropriate to do so. A multi-project lessons learned meeting works where the goals and stakeholder groups of several projects overlap. If there isn't enough overlap to justify having one single meeting, invite attendees for the part of the meeting that is relevant to them. Alternatively, consider running a couple of lessons learned sessions on the same day, so attendees who have contributed to more than one project are able to curate their thoughts for one concerted piece of effort instead of it being spread out over several weeks.

If you have several projects that are closing at similar times, it could be beneficial to run a single meeting where approval is given to close each project. As you look over your calendar and your high-level milestone plan, consider what other meetings it might be possible to combine. There's more on multi-project governance in Chapter 7.

> Right now I'm in the middle of three smaller projects all due within the next month while trying to maintain and keep pushing forward on the major project that is my main job. Luckily there is a lot of crossover with the same stakeholders on multiple projects which makes communication easier – we can catch up on multiple items in the same conversation. One challenge is that I'm so busy running between meetings I'm having a hard time putting my notes down and planning for the next steps, rather than just dashing to the next deadline. I am making an effort to trust my team as much as possible through delegation and leaning out on decision-making until I really need to be involved.
>
> Abigail Appleton, USA

Streamlining project reporting

As Graham Allcott and Hayley Watts say in their book, *How to Fix Meetings* (2021), a culture of good reporting leads to fewer meetings. The more you proactively keep people informed, the fewer meetings stakeholders will need from you.

If you are leading multiple small projects for the same sponsor or manager, then you can combine reporting to make it even easier. Typically, project managers report weekly or monthly, sharing the current status, progress, risks, issues, outstanding decisions, budget situation and anything else that speaks to project performance. Some teams may have a daily standup meeting to take the pulse of the project(s).

Regular written reports can be combined, as can be seen in Table 5.2. Agree core performance items to report against and list these in the first column. Put the project names across the top. If your report recipients will be able to see the report in colour, change the cell background colour to the appropriate Red/Amber/Green status to reflect the summary project status. There's more on RAG colour coding in Chapter 4, but, as a recap, Green would mean the project is progressing to plan, Amber (Yellow) would show it is at risk, and Red shows it needs management attention. This is a very visual way of helping your readers identify the projects they need to pay most attention to.

Reporting on many projects

The more projects you have, the harder it is to prepare consolidated reports that appear meaningful and are still easy to interpret. There's little value in presenting a single slide on each of 20 projects and then expecting the audience to understand which of those projects they should be paying the most attention to. The larger your portfolio of open items, the more work you have to do to highlight where management attention is required.

One way to do this is to first flag projects that have a Red status and need input or decisions from your manager, project sponsor or governance group. Focus on the initiatives that they need to be aware of for their work, because they can positively influence the outcome or remove roadblocks.

Another way to streamline reporting of large amounts of projects is to go back to the portfolio workload spreadsheet you created in Chapter 3 and review the buckets of work. Then report against these buckets, not at individual project level. For example, highlight the key milestones across a bucket of work and report against those to show aggregated progress. Another option would be to identify the organizational benefits that will be achieved across a bucket, flag the contribution of each project and report on how close you are to achieving those benefits.

TABLE 5.2 Sample multi-project status report

Project Name	Web design project	Product launch project	Office relocation project
Summary	Progressing to plan; client satisfied with the wireframes delivered last month and is supporting the next phase of development	Product focus groups were carried out this month and feedback was good. The work continues to plan but is Amber because we have yet to secure premises for manufacture	The move is running two months behind and we will not be able to hit original deadlines
Milestones due this month	1 July: Development complete 27 July: Changes into production	None	Health & safety visit – delayed Decision on artwork – delayed
Milestones due next month	15 August: Demo with client 28 August: Budget approval for next phase	20 August: Secure premises – we have several venues in mind but need to work quickly to arrange a lease on a suitable property to ensure we meet schedule dates	We need to replan the project to establish realistic timeframes for the outstanding work
Top risks & issues	Risk of slippage due to sickness – see below Client contact is on holiday for three weeks during August – may impact decision timetable	Need to secure a location – see above	No solution has been found for the recycling bins issue – with Facilities team to resolve Building is still not available for us to move into

Budget	Total budget (this phase): £75k Spend to date: £60k Estimate to complete: £73k	Budget depends on premises being secured – final costings will be put in the Board Paper due to be discussed on the 10th	Total budget: £550k Spend to date: £325k
Resourcing	The lead web developer is out of the business on sickness absence and this may impact our ability to deliver unless we can source alternative resource	None	We didn't factor in a resource's paternity leave to the schedule, so the office comms is now being managed by the project manager instead of the comms lead, until he returns
Decisions required	Upcoming decision required by client about scope of next phase	Premises selection	None

While project-level reporting may be expected, there is often more organizational value in understanding the impact or contribution of a group of initiatives that deliver results towards a common goal. If you have the time, prepare consolidated reports as well as any individual reports that are mandated by the management team, and see how they respond to seeing the bigger picture.

Creating countdown plans

A countdown plan is a step-by-step guide to what needs to be done by someone (or a team) in order to be ready for the launch or go live for a project. Not all projects are going to need a countdown plan, but they are a useful resource if your project involves:

- Process change;
- Internal policy change;
- Changes to working practices or expectations of staff;
- Data migration, for example where historical information needs to be transferred into a new software product;
- User training.

In all these cases, team leaders or individuals need to take responsibility for their part in being ready for the incoming changes, and the countdown plan helps with that. The countdown plan can be a simple spreadsheet with columns for:

- Tasks;
- Owner;
- Due date;
- Status;
- Notes.

The list of data points to include is similar to the project schedules and timelines created as part of managing the project. The difference is that a countdown plan is a very simple checklist or To Do list for people who are not used to looking at things 'the project management way'. They would benefit from a simple list that focuses purely on what they have to do.

Each team or department affected will take your countdown plan template and use it as a working guide as the go live date for the project moves closer. You will create it for them, but they will take responsibility for updating it. It includes activities they will do and also what will be done for them. Examples of tasks that could be included are:

- Book a meeting room for the project kick-off meeting for that department.
- Nominate a change champion or local lead for this project.
- Provide a list of PC reference numbers/logins that need access to the new software.
- Agree dates for training.
- Put up posters in staff area.
- Cascade training materials to the whole team, keeping a list of who attends.
- Organize delivery of resources and keep them on site until the project team arrives to install them.

There is an example in Table 5.3.

Creating a countdown plan for each department affected by your project is a change management activity; if you have a change manager assigned to the project, then they can take this on. However, I've never had a dedicated business change manager on any of my smaller projects, because if your organization has people in that role they are normally tied up supporting large-scale organizational change. As the project manager of many smaller projects, you are likely to need to do this yourself.

It is an additional task when you are already feeling busy and overwhelmed but the payoff is immense. The easier you can make it for someone else to do their parts of the project, and the more you can help them prioritize their project tasks, the less you have to support them in the future.

TABLE 5.3 Example countdown plan

				Countdown Plan for HR Department Go Live		
#	Task	Owner	Due Date	Status	Find more information	Notes
1	Book meeting room for project kickoff meeting	[name]	[date]	Complete		Team manager + HR manager to attend, plus others identified by team manager
2	Nominate change champion	[name]	[date]	In progress		Need to confirm asap
3	Provide list of PCs to IT including user IDs	[name]	[date]	To do		
4	Agree dates for training	[name]	[date]	To do		
5	Book meeting rooms for training	[name]	[date]	To do		
6	Deliver briefing to all team	[name]	[date]	To do	Use the slides on the central drive (link)	
7	Read training manual	[name]	[date]	To do	Project manager will send you the manual	Call me if you don't have it by month end

One week to go						
8	Check all the user logins work	[name]	[date]	To do		
9	Share the briefing with the team	[name]	[date]	To do	Link to be provided	Still being approved by legal
10	Review planned staff absence	[name]	[date]	To do		Organize extra staff to be on site if needed
11	Go/no go decision	[name]	[date]	To do	Call details to be provided	
Go live!						
12	Be on site between 8am–8pm	[name]	[date]	To do	Project team will be with you	
13	Put up balloons and banners	[name]	[date]	On hold		Budget to be confirmed
14	Catered lunch to be provided by project team	[name]	[date]	To do		Please provide dietary needs
15	Put out desk drops on each desk before 9am	[name]	[date]	To do		
16	Dial in for CEO's message at 4pm	[name]	[date]	To do	Meeting details to be provided	

You'll still want to check in and make sure they are on track and doing what the countdown plan says, but you can use that document as your main communication, which limits the amount of additional communication materials you'll need to provide for them.

They will feel more engaged with the project, they will understand the process and they will hopefully stop feeling overwhelmed themselves with the changes coming their way. They will be able to proactively engage with the project and take ownership of the things that fall to them. It's also a good way of holding people accountable and making sure they are on track with dates. It minimizes the number of distractions involved in engaging with the project by breaking down their work into really small steps.

It may feel like this document is basically spoon-feeding professionals what they should already know how to do, but everyone is busy. It's easier for you to use a template to create a countdown plan for them instead of them trying to work it out themselves. Once they understand what they have to do, the goal is for you to be a little bit more hands-off because you have already set them up for success.

Creating a communication calendar

If your project affects a number of teams, you will need to let them know what's going on. Often, you can do that by briefing team leaders and having them cascade information to their teams. That saves you time, but risks the message not being transmitted exactly as you would like.

Where there are several projects affecting the same group of teams, it makes sense to consolidate information so team leaders have an easier job of sharing what their colleagues need to know. That's where a consolidated communications plan comes into play. A consolidated approach is a way to minimize stakeholder overwhelm, by combining communications where it makes sense to do so. Look for the points where it makes sense to run communications together to make it easier for everyone.

The first step in creating a consolidated communications calendar is to check that you have a communications schedule for each project.

What is being shared with whom, and when is it being shared? Your communication points for individual projects may include:

- Staff presentations;
- Newsletter articles;
- Updates on the intranet or via collaboration tools;
- Written briefings;
- Formal reports.

Make a list of key dates and planned communications for each project. A table works well for this: list the next six months down the side and the project names across the top. Then plot what comms are being created and shared for each project in each month.

The goal is to get a sense of what's being sent to whom and when, so you can try to minimize duplication and avoid overlaps. It can also help you see where your stakeholders might be busy. For example, if one group is having training on a new business process for Project 1 during May, it might be too much for them to also learn about a new software tool you are launching for Project 2 at the same time. Or it might align perfectly, and you can combine the training to cover both.

Look at when you're sending out information to the same group of people. Can you put that into one consolidated project newsletter, perhaps coming from the Project Management Office if you have one? Could you create a form that asks for two sets of inputs instead of just one, to meet the requirements for data collection for two of your projects? Have a think about where you could use and combine your information. Could you include updates on a couple of projects in a staff briefing instead of using the time for just one? It won't be possible to combine or consolidate every aspect of your communication but do it where you can.

One important aspect of project communications is making decisions. As a project team, you'll make a lot of decisions about what to do and how to do it. When you have multiple projects on the go, you need a way of recording decisions to remove the burden of remembering them all.

I learned to keep a decision log. When you are designing buildings, you make decisions or the client makes decisions, on the scope, timing or on the budget. I find it is important to keep track of which decisions are taken, why and by whom so that later on you can refer to that. I have a list of decisions with dates and the project phase as an almost chronological record of when things were decided. That's something I learned the hard way to do.

Els, architect, Belgium

A decision log is a simple record of:

- What decision was made, written as a statement;
- Who made the decision;
- The date the decision was taken;
- A link to where there is more information, such as meeting minutes or a recommendation paper.

The value of the decision log is only clear when someone asks why a decision was taken… and you can't remember! Look it up and explain why that choice was made. If necessary, the decision can be overturned or changed if new information becomes available or the project takes a different direction. However, that should be done with consideration for the rationale used in the past, and in a controlled way.

These five ways of working – combining meetings and reporting, creating countdown plans and communication calendars, and recording decisions – will help you streamline project communications and make it easier to engage with stakeholders across multiple projects at the same time.

You won't need or want to use all the tools and techniques discussed in this chapter on every project. People are as dynamic as the situations they find themselves in, so test out approaches for engagement and see what works for your particular project, your office culture, your environment and the stakeholders themselves.

It might work to combine project status meetings for one sponsor, but another wants you to stick to separate meetings for each project. Or they might change their mind a few months later and ask you to combine your updates into one conversation.

Keep monitoring what is working and giving you and your project team the best results. Do more of what works, but be aware that as your project moves forward, so too do your relationships. If you notice engagement is flagging, try switching up what you do as that might give the team a boost.

Making the most of time with other people

A large part of engaging people is getting the time to speak to them, and that is not always easy. Therefore, when you do get in front of them, you want to make the most of the time you have together. As everyone is different, the methods you use to meet up and work with colleagues will be different. Some people will want face-to-face time if they can have it. Others will be happy with a quick status update via text message. Different situations will demand different types and lengths of interaction. Being productive when you work with stake-holders is going to look different for each engagement, so let's consider some ways to get the most out of whatever time you have with stakeholders.

> If you have attention issues, staying tuned in the entire time is exhausting so you want the freedom to zoom out from time to time to save your attention for what matters.
>
> Agendas help, especially if they have time next to each of the agenda items. Not that it will be religiously kept to but to have some kind of idea when each item will be discussed, where it's possible.
>
> People that are neurodiverse also tend to be socially clumsy so if you have multiple people trying to give feedback they might not know how to break into the conversation. The project manager can help by making it clear what the protocol is for getting your contribution in and how you make it be known that you have something to add.

There's a rhythm to a conversation and if you have difficulty with time, you have difficulty with timing. It might be difficult to spot the pauses. Then by the time you figure out what you want to say, the pause is gone.

Brian R King, neurodiversity productivity coach, USA

Book shorter meetings

All your stakeholders are busy. One thing you can do to make the most of their time is to cut the duration of meetings. Many calendar software tools have a default length of time for a meeting. The one I use defaults each meeting to one hour, and most people use the default setting. You don't have to. Change the default duration of meetings to 45 minutes. You can still get through an hour's worth of meeting conversation and agenda topics in 45 minutes because you will be more targeted, focused and waste less time.

If your stakeholders don't buy into the idea of shorter meetings, book the meeting for an hour and then finish it 15 minutes early. If 15 minutes is too much of a stretch, aim to cut ten minutes off the end of the meeting. That gives you some time to catch your breath between meetings or complete a couple of the small tasks that dropped out of your last conversations.

Alternatively, start your meetings at ten past the hour. People will soon get used to it! Try a few different varieties of meeting times and see what works best for you.

Some people are not interested in coming to meetings, or are too busy to come to meetings, but you still need their input. Reach out to them in different formats. In my experience, text-based conversation has been an effective way of working with technical teams. If they are always chatting away in their messaging tool, maybe that's the channel to meet them on. The right communication approach will save you (and them) some time.

Jen Mckay, HR coordinator, USA

Schedule at 80 per cent availability

Project management software allows team members to assign themselves or other people to particular activities. That is resource scheduling: making sure people are available to do the work at the required time and that no one is overloaded or sitting around with nothing to do.

It is tempting to think that everyone on the team, yourself included, has a full work day to commit to project tasks. Let's say that a software engineer allocates one day a week to one of your projects. They work 9am to 5pm so that's a full seven hours of work, because they are entitled to take an hour's lunch break. However, they are unlikely to do seven hours of productive work in that time. It is more realistic to set expectations of working time at 80 per cent of available time because of interruptions, bathroom breaks, needing to do errands, fixing the printer because paper is jammed... and everything else that means you are not pumping out productive work for a straight seven hours.

The 80 per cent rule is not a strict expectation. Consider it a guideline that helps you get to a more realistic portioning of time. When you use the 80 per cent rule, you are building in natural contingency time and hopefully have more chance of hitting your project deadlines while not burning out your team.

Use a two-week look ahead

A two-week look ahead is a regular planning conversation with the team where you discuss what is going to happen in the next fortnight and what might make those things harder to achieve. It's a quick meeting where you ask questions like:

- Do we all know what the priorities are for the next fortnight?
- What do we need to be doing now to be ready for these activities in a fortnight?
- What might stop us from hitting the deadlines due in a fortnight?

- What hasn't been finished yet that needs to be carried forward into the next fortnight, and how does that affect our planned work?
- Is anyone out of the office in the next fortnight or unable to work on this particular project during that time?
- Do we need to adjust our schedule to make sure people are available, given what we know now?
- What other projects have we got on that might affect our work in the next fortnight?
- What have we learned recently that could shape or influence our work going forward?

Use the time with the team to review how things are going and to make sure that realistic expectations are set for the upcoming two-week period.

Find out when people are available

If your organization uses a shared calendar system, use that to your advantage. You can check the busy/available times for your colleagues, and sometimes even see where they are going to be, depending on the privacy level and settings they have chosen for their account. Put a note in your calendar to remind you to make calls when you can see your stakeholders look like they might be free.

People who travel for work might be available to take calls while they are waiting for trains or flights, as long as the conversation does not require them to disclose confidential information which they would not be comfortable talking about in a public place. When I travelled internationally for work, I would make a lot of calls from the airport as there wasn't much else productive I could do. Talk to their executive assistant and find out when would be a good time to call. Be strategic about when you get in touch with your colleagues and you are more likely to reach them when they are able to respond in a timely manner.

Watch when people send their emails. I was working with an international team, and a colleague would send emails that arrived with me at 1am or 2am in the morning, my time. Another colleague based in Mumbai would send emails that arrived around 4am. I watched the times that they would send emails so I would know when I would be most likely to get hold of them or to get a fast response. I could work out when they were available, typically working and looking through their list of To Dos, and then I could schedule my messages to send then.

Dr Una Olmstead, USA

Paying attention to people's schedules also works the other way: note when people tend to gravitate to you for help. Is there a time in the day or week when you seem to get interrupted more often? When are your phone and collaboration tools constantly pinging with incoming calls or messages? Pre-empt those times by keeping your diary light or doing work where you can be easily interrupted. Alternatively, walk around the office or check in with your colleagues with a quick chat message to find out if they have anything for you before you settle in for a period of focused work.

When people are available is part of the equation, but how to reach them is also important. Phone calls and emails are options, and most stakeholders will have many other ways to reach them, like collaboration tools, or text or voice messages on various platforms. Ask your colleagues how they would prefer you to get in touch with them. What's the channel they are most connected to, the one they gravitate to and use the most? That's the best way to get in touch. While you are having the conversation, point out what works best for you too, in case they need to get hold of you urgently.

I worked out that 8.30am is the best time to drop in somebody's inbox, because that makes your message the first thing they see in the morning. Or if they've been on holiday, I time the message to arrive for 10am. At that point they've probably got through their urgent stuff and are ready, sitting with a second cup of tea ready to get back into work.

Amanda Howard, project manager, higher education sector, UK

Make the time to build relationships

The single biggest thing you can do to make the most of time with other people is to have a trusted professional relationship with them. When you have that, you can dive straight into the heart of any conversation. You can provide a different level of background information because they will already have confidence that you are presenting everything they need to know.

Investing time in building those relationships will pay off many times over. Put people at the centre of your projects, not the tasks, activities or goals. Make your workplace inclusive. Use strategies that allow everyone to contribute. That will help you communicate and collaborate effectively, as well as encouraging feelings of belonging in the team. It also supports resilience in the team: people are more likely to be patient and work with you to address challenges if they trust you are doing the best job you can with the information and resources you have.

Relationship building goes faster when you meet people face-to-face. Budget – if you can – for remote teams to meet up at the beginning of a new piece of work. That will help everyone get to know each other and show that you are willing to invest time and effort in developing those relationships for the good for the project. Where it is impossible to meet in person, think about how you can foster a sense of team and stay connected to each other despite the distance.

> For the last six years, I have managed multiple projects at a time. It is hard to keep up if you don't have a good platform to track progress and a good schedule system to manage meetings and deadlines. I believe that the key to succeed in managing multiple projects is learning how to build a good team in a culture of trust where you can delegate important tasks and trust that the work is getting done. Early in all my projects, I make sure that we are building the right foundation for the project by meeting with the sponsor, stakeholders and teams and listen to why the project is important, clearly defining their roles and working together on setting clear expectations.
>
> Ana Lozoya, IT PMO manager, Canada

KEY TAKEAWAYS

- Stakeholder engagement is the activity that keeps people connected to your projects. The more people feel connected to your project, the less chasing up you should (hopefully) have to do, saving you time.

- Project sponsors are the most influential of all your stakeholders.

- The stakeholder directory and stakeholder map are your tools for understanding who is involved in which projects, so no one gets forgotten.

- You have limited time, so prioritize working with and engaging the most appropriate stakeholders in the most time-efficient ways to get the best results for the project.

- Setting expectations helps you manage the work and helps others know what they have to do.

- Streamlining project communications through consolidated reporting, meetings and other communications helps to avoid stakeholder overload and helps people deal with all the changes an organization is going through – not just the one project you're talking about at the moment.

ACTION STEPS

Your action steps from this chapter are:

- Identify all your stakeholders and create a stakeholder register and stakeholder map.

- Review the power, legitimacy and expectation of urgency of your stakeholders across all of your projects, and use a table to identify stakeholder saliency and to help you prioritize where you spend your time.

- Check everyone knows what is expected of them for each project and that they are only scheduled to work at 80 per cent of their available hours.

- Review your upcoming meetings and see what can be combined and which ones can be done in less time: change your default meeting time to at least ten minutes less than what it is now.

- Look at your individual communications plans and see where it makes sense to consolidate and merge the information that is being shared with your stakeholders.

References

Association for Project Management (2019) *APM Body of Knowledge*, 7th edn, APM, Princes Risborough

Allcott, G and Watts, H (2021) *How to Fix Meetings*, Icon Books, London

Gallup, Inc (2020) *The Relationship Between Engagement at Work and Organizational Outcomes, 2020 Q12® Meta-Analysis*: 10th edn. Available from www.gallup.com/workplace/321725/gallup-q12-meta-analysis-report.aspx (archived at https://perma.cc/9PAN-8Q4A)

Gallup, Inc (2021) *State of the Global Workplace 2021 Report*. Available from www.gallup.com/workplace/349484/state-of-the-global-workplace.aspx (archived at https://perma.cc/CBT8-XQHA)

Harrin, E (2020) *Engaging Stakeholders on Projects: How to harness people power*, APM, Princes Risborough

Harrin, E (2021) Managing multiple projects: the research, 29 October. Available from https://rebelsguidetopm.com/managing-multiple-projects-the-research/ (archived at https://perma.cc/73XE-MV4Z)

Mitchell, R K, Agle, B R and Wood, D J (1997) Toward a theory of stakeholder identification and salience: Defining the principle of who and what really counts, *The Academy of Management Review*, 22 (4), 853–86

Nieto-Rodriguez, A (2021) *Harvard Business Review Project Management Handbook: How to launch, lead and sponsor successful projects*, Harvard Business Review Press, Boston

Further reading

Pullan, P (2016) *Virtual Leadership*, Kogan Page, London

Smith, T and Kirby, A (2021) *Neurodiversity at Work: Drive innovation, performance and productivity with a neurodiverse workforce*, Kogan Page, London

Concept #4: Productivity: managing your own time

Managing multiple projects is a lot like juggling: you have a lot of balls in the air and it's important each of them stays moving. You could easily spend all your time working on one project, to the detriment of others. However, the reality for most people with a multi-project workload is that you have to make progress (and be seen to be making progress) across all your projects, because that is what your customers expect.

It's often said that you can't manage time. Time passes whether you want it to or not. We can only make the best of the time we have by making sure we are working on the right things and dedicating our focus to the activities that matter most. That's harder than it sounds. In a study for their book, *Not Today*, Erica and Mike Schultz (2021) found that 47 per cent of respondents spend a significant amount of work time on non-value added tasks or timewasting activities.

It is also hard to stay focused with the constant distractions at work. In a survey by Udemy (2018), 50 per cent of people reported being significantly less productive as a result of distractions, with 74 per cent of millennials and Gen Z respondents describing themselves as distracted at work. The impacts are significant: lack of motivation, stress, frustration and decreased staff retention, and – according to research carried out by Mark et al (2008) – compensating for interruptions by working faster.

If you have several projects on the go at once you will end up switching between them during the week, and often during a single day, as you focus on what is currently important. Being productive in such an environment is the fourth concept in the managing multiple projects framework, as shown in Figure 6.1. A key skill is being able to make the most of your working hours so you keep everything moving forward – without leaving you feeling overwhelmed or burnt out. Having a toolbox full of productivity and time management strategies will help you maximize your time.

This chapter is your toolbox. You'll learn about the productivity saboteurs that stop you making progress and how to overcome them. You'll discover new tips to boost your productivity and techniques to help keep you focused on the most important tasks.

FIGURE 6.1   The Productivity concept in the managing multiple projects framework

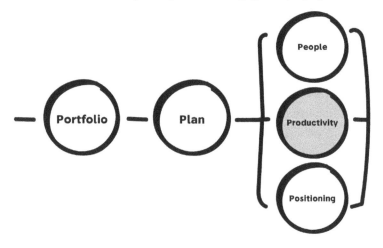

Productivity saboteurs

Research for this book (Harrin, 2021) shows that over a third of project managers find procrastination their largest productivity saboteur when it comes to managing multiple projects, as shown in Figure 6.2. Productivity can be affected by many things. There are plenty of things at work that make it hard for you to progress your projects – the skill is in being able to identify and tackle them so you can keep moving forward. Let's look at the top productivity saboteurs identified in Figure 6.2: procrastination, disorganization and poor planning, and how you can effectively address each of these.

Procrastination

Procrastination can be characterized by general dithering about, putting off tasks and choosing to work on other things because they are easier or shorter, and not making progress. Humans seem to be wired to find easy ways to do things, and sometimes doing a completely different task is easier than the big, difficult thing you've got at the top of your To Do list. As one survey respondent wrote, their biggest productivity saboteur is 'Prioritizing items and doing the easy things first.'

> Procrastination tends to be the evil of productivity. Whether this is a big or small task/project, we tend to leave the bigger ones which causes the procrastination within us. Why? Because we feel it takes a lot longer. So we focus on the small ones. If you calculated the time it took to do the smaller tasks this would almost equate to the same time it would take the bigger projects. So why not flip this on its head and use procrastination to your advantage? Procrastinate on the small tasks which don't really matter and work on the bigger tasks. Bigger projects may require quality and we aim for perfection. But focus on 'Version One Is Better Than Version None' and progress to high quality. The surprising thing is the smaller tasks you have left aside may no longer need doing, because they have been covered in the bigger projects. So use procrastination to your advantage and flip it over to the smaller projects/tasks. Use procrastination to increase your productivity, and you be in control rather than letting it control you.
>
> Chet Hirani, performance coach, UK

FIGURE 6.2   Productivity saboteurs identified by project managers

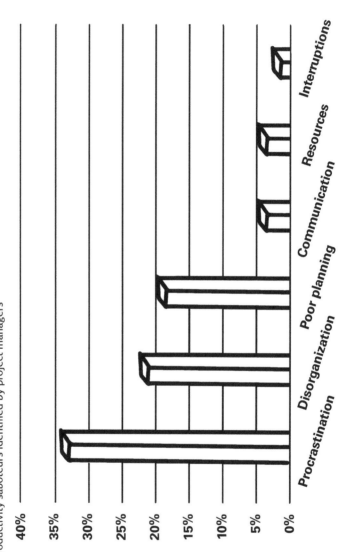

If it feels like procrastinating is a challenge you share, here are some tips for managing procrastination. First, get clear on the vision and the goals for your projects. Write them down and stick them up near your desk. Being able to visually see where you are going and what your targets are can help you stay on track.

Make the most of your calendar. Plan your time so you have blocks of hours available to work on certain things. Use colour coding to help keep you on track. There's more about personal time management and time blocking later in this chapter, so keep reading for tips for how to use your calendar effectively.

Make sure you get enough sleep. It's really hard to do anything if you don't have enough sleep. You'll fall into the habit of doing the easy work because you don't have the cognitive capacity to deal with anything that takes strategic thinking or a bit of brainpower. Eating is just as important. You'll know how your body reacts without food: skipping lunch is rarely a good idea, especially if it makes you cranky.

Interruptions and distractions were only the major productivity saboteur for 2 per cent of project managers in my research for this book, but we all suffer from them. Identify what interrupts or distracts you the most and how you could better respond to those. For example:

- Social media: unless it's part of your job, put time aside to check and participate on social media.
- Phone calls: screen your calls. Record an out of office message and if you don't recognize the number, let it go to voicemail and attend to it later.
- Email: set an out of office message and take an afternoon off being constantly in your inbox, or dedicate time slots during the day to reading and responding to messages.

Break your big tasks into smaller ones. Procrastination often happens when people find it difficult to make progress on something because it feels too big. If you can break the work down into smaller activities, you might find it easier to make some progress.

Finally, focus on the consequences of not doing something. There might not be any consequences, in which case, you have to ask yourself, why am I spending time on this? However, there are probably going to be substantive consequences for you and for your project if the work doesn't get done. If you're aware of those, that could give you a little bit of pressure for making sure that you make time to do your tasks.

ONE, TWO, DONE

Get into the habit of 'one, two, done': this means touch something one time, and if it's a task you can complete in under two minutes, it gets done straight away. For example, a quick response to an email, booking a meeting, filing a document, leaving a voicemail (only if you can guarantee they won't pick up, as that would push it over two minutes).

David Allen popularized the two-minute rule in his book *Getting Things Done* (2002). The key is to only apply the rule if you are already doing something related to the task. For example, you're in your inbox, sorting out a lot of emails and one needs a quick response. That's an OK situation to apply 'one, two, done'. If you are working through your inbox sorting emails and suddenly remember you need to take mail to the post box (or post room) then pause before you get up from your desk. While the mail drop task might only take two minutes, it would pull you away from what you are currently doing so it's not a good use of your time. Allen calls the time you spend working out what to do with each activity 'processing time' and this is when it makes most sense to apply the two-minute rule. Where it takes longer to schedule the task than to do it now, doing it now is your best choice. Note down any unrelated tasks so you don't forget them and come back to them later.

Disorganization

As we saw in Figure 6.2, over one in five project managers report their biggest productivity saboteur is being disorganized. Given that being organized is pretty much a key skill for someone managing projects, that might come as a surprise. However, when things are busy at work, corners are cut – often with good intentions. Later, that causes problems because the task wasn't completed in exactly the right way.

> While I was creating a new project management webinar, I saved files to a variety of places. Slides went in the 'Speaking' folder, handouts for delegates went in my 'Products to Download' folder, promotional information went somewhere else, and I saved the video recording on to a hard drive.
>
> Needless to say, when I wanted to re-run the webinar, it took a while to find all the different components. A disorganized filing system (even though it felt like it made sense at the time) slowed me down.

Being disorganized leads to not being able to find important information in a timely fashion. It can contribute to missing deadlines, because you didn't remember, or didn't know, they were coming. It can result in turning up late for meetings, not working on the right things, or duplicating tasks that someone else has already completed. I'm sure we have all worked with people who are the epitome of disorganization. Whether that is you or whether that is somebody in your team, there are some things that you can do to help and resolve disorganization as one of your productivity saboteurs.

First, consider your calendar as your friend. Create alerts and notifications to act as reminders. For example, Outlook defaults to reminding you of meetings 15 minutes in advance, but you can set yourself a reminder for two or three days in advance. Use that, for example, as a prompt to send out a meeting agenda.

Next, try to create a structured environment in which to work. You don't have to do that all in one go. Start small, and build in structure as and when you have time or are picking up a task to do. For example:

- The next time you need the contact details of a key supplier, create a contacts list in a tool of your choice and put them in there. Add the contact details for other stakeholders or vendors in time.

- The next time you need to file an email, quickly review where it's going to end up. Is the folder name clear? Will you be able to find it again? And do you need to keep it at all? A better answer might be to save any attachments and delete the original email. Decide on your approach for email filing and stick to it going forward. Don't worry about re-filing everything from the past – just use your new personal rules going forward.

- Choose one method for taking notes and stick to it, whether that's a notebook, an app, dictation which you transcribe, or something else.

In my experience, a lot of the feelings of overwhelm and disorganization stem from technology. Modern collaboration tools are designed to be intuitive and need little training, and unfortunately that has meant that employees are often left to their own devices to work out how to effectively use the tools they are given. While you can pick up the basics with very little learning curve, there are often helpful shortcuts and best practices available – if only you knew about them.

Block out ten minutes every couple of weeks to review the help files available from your project management software tool provider. Most products have both video and text-based user guides so you can learn how to use the software more effectively. If time is a premium (and when is it not?), play the training videos on 1.5 speed. Being able to confidently use your software tools can make the difference between feeling like data is lost forever and being able to quickly save and retrieve important information, and stay more organized.

FILING FOR FINDING

Filing for finding means storing information in a way that makes it easy to find in the future. Think about how your document filing system is set up. Simple changes, like numbering folders or creating naming conventions for documents, will make it easier to retrieve files in the future. For example:

- Number folders if you want them to appear in a certain order. Naming folders 01 – January, 02 – February and so on will ensure they appear in the right order. Do the same with 01 – Project initiation, 02 – Planning and other topics if you have folders for project stages.

- Use the year-month-date format for dates in file names to enable files to be sorted by name and appear in chronological order, for example 'Project Board Minutes 20220606' for the notes of a meeting from 6 June 2022.

- Pay attention to file names from scanned files, photographs or attachments. These often default to random characters, dates, 'Doc1' and so on. Change names to match your naming convention.

Poor planning

Figure 6.2 shows that poor planning is the productivity saboteur that 20 per cent of project managers find the biggest challenge. It results in having to do rework, and causing confusion because you're not exactly sure where to start, so you might start on something that's not the right task for now. Poor planning can really affect how much progress you're making.

Verbatim survey responses for the impact and causes of poor planning:

- Rework or wasted work due to competing project priorities
- Things often take longer than expected
- Too many competing priorities
- Prioritization of which issues to focus on and which to leave to the teams to solve
- Other people's lack of planning and procrastination becoming someone else's emergency
- Lack of clearly defined and approved requirements from the business areas
- Lack of clear strategy or vision from senior management
- Lack of clarity on project requirements which leads to rework
- Lack of clarity from project sponsor, frequent scope evolution

- Bad memory – too many balls juggling in the air and I drop a ball and then forget I ever had it.

Unsurprisingly, the fix for poor planning is to plan. One of the common barriers to creating a plan is the knowledge that it will change. What's the point in investing time in planning if your workload and calendar will look different next week?

It is worth planning – at least at a level of detail that won't make you deflate like a popped balloon when someone changes their mind about an activity. You know your environment and your stakeholders: if you know that you won't be able to bring more stability to the setting, then instead focus on how to adapt quickly and make nimble changes to your plan as the situation evolves. Take a look at the section on rolling wave planning in Chapter 4 for some guidance on how to document a project when you aren't sure of exactly what is going to be worked on at any given time, but stakeholders still want to see that you have 'a plan'.

Ideally, you would be able to influence your environment to bring a bit more stability to the work. This might take a few difficult conversations with internal customers or senior leaders to highlight the challenges of trying to get things done when everything changes.

Another approach is to work with your team, if you have one, to create a plan that you can all buy into. Often plans fail because the right people were not involved in creating them. You've probably been in a situation where someone tells you what needs to happen by when: it's not a good feeling because it removes your agency. This impact on motivation and commitment may be the difference between hitting a date and not hitting it, so if you can encourage others to tell you when their pieces of the project will be completed, that's a starting point for your scheduling. If project team members offer you dates that do not fit with overall expectations, or they refuse to commit to dates at all, that's a different challenge!

TIPS FOR WHEN PEOPLE WON'T COMMIT TO DATES

One of the biggest challenges for people managing projects is getting their colleagues to commit to delivery dates for their portions of the work – and then ensuring those dates are achieved. If you find people will not commit to dates the issues could be:

- They don't know how to estimate: help them break down the task into smaller chunks and work out how long it will take.

- They don't know how to deal with the uncertainty: ask them what the major risks to their work would be and what would stop them achieving those dates. Then factor that into the estimate. For example, talk about best case/worst case scenarios and put the worst case dates on your schedule (while hoping they meet the best case dates).

- They don't understand that their work has an impact on anything else: show them the overall plan and explain the consequences to the project overall if their tasks are not completed on time.

- Their manager is not prioritizing the project tasks and letting them have time to work on them: explain the value, relevance and importance of the project so they can share that with their manager and, if necessary, escalate to their manager or your project sponsor.

Agree a process for dealing with changes to that plan, as next week it might look totally different. The process should be a way for the team to assess and incorporate new requests and changes. That allows you to adapt and iterate as you go – but it needs to be a process followed by everyone. Make sure stakeholders know how to suggest changes and guide them through the approval process so they can be incorporated into the plan in a structured way, where everyone knows their impact.

Consider how you are working together as a team. Is your approach keeping everyone on the same page? You can do that through regular conversations, one to one check-ins, team meetings, and any other communications that you push out to people. Communication can really help by making sure that everybody knows what the priorities are for the upcoming week based on what your plan says.

Overcoming the saboteurs

A lot of issues with productivity are actually issues with mindset. Your working style can be changed if you want it to change. Give yourself permission to be more organized – sometimes disorganization is a learned habit. If you can get out of the habit and try to set yourself up with systems, then you can perhaps be more efficient with how you make things work.

Everyone works and thinks in different ways. Try different approaches, test and iterate, and ditch what doesn't work for you. I take notes in a notebook, but that might be inefficient for you. You will find something that works, so get creative and use your tech to the best advantage to make systems work for you.

Techniques to make the most of your time

Work time is split between the time you spend with other people in meetings or working together, which is covered in Chapter 5, and the time you spend doing your own work independently of others. Making the most of both those types of time will help you feel more productive and on top of your workload.

One way to filter tasks coming in is to use what Canfield et al (2000) call the 4-D solution: dump (which I call delete in this digital world), delegate, defer, do. In other words, you have four choices for every task that comes across your desk:

- Delete: no one needs to do this task. Make the decision that it is not going to get done.

- Delegate: the task needs to be done, but not necessarily by you. Delegate it to the person best placed to complete it. If you don't know who could do it, but know that you don't want to or don't have time to do it, ask who else is available to pick the work up. You may need to make a note to follow up (which is a task for your personal To Do list).

- Defer: the task needs to be done by you. It's not something you can do right now, so schedule it or make a note that it needs to be done at some point.

- Do: the task needs to be done by you. If it's appropriate to do it now, do so. If it can't be done now, put it on your To Do list, noting its relative priority, even if that means something else has to drop off.

Time is precious. We can only make the most of what we have. Practise making quick decisions as you look through your list of incoming requests.

> People with time blindness don't feel time passing so they have difficulty estimating how long things are going to take. When you hear about people who put off things to the last minute and burn the midnight oil, these are usually people who think, 'I've got enough time'. For them the future is always far away until it feels like it's right here because their sense of time is either 'now' or 'not now', there isn't a sense of progression. We have a funny relationship with the clock. We have half an hour to do something and our body doesn't know what half an hour feels like.
>
> I always have a clock in front of me on the upper right-hand corner of the computer screen. I use Google calendar so it has the scrolling bar on the calendar to show me where I am in the day. The Time Timer, which was built for kids in the classroom, shows time as a big red pie and as time lessens, the red goes away. By showing time as a decreasing amount of red that computes with the brain to register that time is dwindling. So having concrete measures can really help. In some cases, you have to set yourself multiple alarms, sometimes every 15 minutes.
>
> A lot of people who are working well in teams could have flown under the radar and don't necessarily know why they do things differently so they might not have insight into time blindness.
>
> Brian R. King, neurodiversity productivity coach, USA

TIS: Task, Interest, Skill

Once tasks have made it on to your To Do list, another way of maximizing your available time is to use what I call Task/Interest/Skill (TIS) to come up with the best way to approach each activity.

Ask yourself:

- What is the task?
- What is your level of interest in the task?
- How skilled are you at doing the task?

This information helps you establish your profile for each task and how you might best make the most of your time tackling it. There are four task profiles as shown in Figure 6.3.

FIGURE 6.3   Task profiles

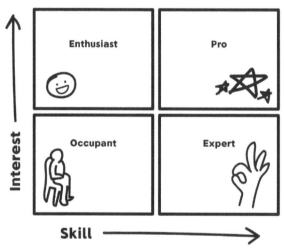

Occupant: For these tasks you have low interest and low skill. The tasks occupy you, but you aren't particularly keen to do them or particularly good at them. Spending too much time on tasks that fall into this category will suck your motivation. When you aren't interested in your work and don't know how to get started, you are at risk of procrastinating. Manage these tasks by limiting how many of them you have to do. If the work is crucial to your role, increase your skill level with some training so you can get through them faster. Alternatively, consider delegating the work to somebody who does enjoy that kind of task.

Expert: For these tasks you have low interest and high skill. You are capable of doing the work to a good standard, but it doesn't inspire you. You're considered a safe pair of hands for this work. People know you can do the tasks, but you may find your role boring if too much of your time is spent here. Consider training someone else to do the task: share your knowledge with someone who would love to know how to do it. If a lot of your work falls into this category, it might be time to talk to your manager about a career change or promotion. Resentment may set in if you don't enjoy the tasks that you are being asked to do on a regular basis.

Enthusiast: For these tasks you have high interest and low skill. You enjoy the work but you don't have any special talent at doing it (yet). Tasks in this category can eat up far more time than you originally allowed because once you start them, you begin to research and learn to fill your knowledge gaps. The learning part is fun, so the time passes quickly. Manage these tasks by giving yourself a set window in which to work on them so you can get stuck into improving your skills but limit your ability to get carried away. It's not a good use of your time to get sucked into a new topic when you are pushed for time, so ring fence your time, delegate the work to someone who can do it more quickly than you, or plan to come back to it later when your priority work is done. If time isn't an issue, feel free to spend lots of it on these activities! If you love the work and are learning new skills, one day you'll become a pro.

Pro: For these tasks you have high skill and high interest. You love the work and you are good at it. This is where the state of Flow sets in. This state, described by Mihaly Csikszentmihalyi in his 2002 book called *Flow*, is where you are absorbed in your work, fully immersed in what you are doing and enjoying it – and you look at the clock and three hours have passed without you realizing, during which you've achieved a lot. Achieving a Flow state is a great way to maximize what you can do with your time. Extremely productive people are 2.6 times more likely to work in a state of flow, and 3.8 times more likely to concentrate for longer periods than other people (Schultz and Schultz, 2021).

Try to spend as much time as possible doing pro-level tasks. It's an efficient use of your time because you are skilled at the activities. You'll be doing your best work and enjoying it at the same time. It would be great if your whole working day was full of tasks that found you in a state of Flow and let you act as a pro for hours at a time. However, your workload is going to include other activities that you aren't so good at or care so much about. As someone in charge of multiple projects, there are going to be tasks that need to get done regardless of how much you aren't interested in doing them. Ideally, you'd be able to build a project team to fill your gaps: surround yourself with people who are good at what you are not good at, so together you have an amazing pro profile to tackle the project. In real life you won't always have the ability to recruit or even select people for your team. Look at the Task/Interest/Skill combination for each activity and make a decision about how to approach the work based on your task profile, so you can spend your time as wisely as possible.

Planning time to do your own work

You've carefully curated what you say yes to and considered your levels of interest and skill for each activity so you can use broad strategies make the most of your time. Beyond that, it is helpful to have a toolbox of quick tips and tactics for finding time in your calendar to get your own tasks done. If you're in a lot of meetings, or if you feel that your calendar is out of control, then hopefully some of these tips will help you.

Transfer key dates to your calendar

Transfer key project dates and times to your calendar. Add your team members' holidays and other out of office time as well so you are reminded about their availability. It's also nice to record their birthdays where they are willing to share that information with you, so you can celebrate as a team.

Add a reminder to alert you a couple of days before an important date. Block time in your diary to prepare for those key events; for example, sending out the agenda for a project board meeting, preparing your expenses or a budget report to submit for a project, or completing monthly reporting for your project management office.

Those blocks of time can move if something else comes up, but the fact that they are in there at all will help you preserve the time required to do the work. If you are worried about how it looks to others to have time blocked out on your calendar for personal work and meeting prep, then call it something else. Allcott and Watts suggest you label the time as 'Project Magenta' in their book, *How to Fix Meetings* (2021). Your colleagues won't know what that is, but because it sounds important they won't book their meetings over it either.

Make sure your work calendar is synced with your personal calendar. You have one life, so use one diary system to manage it all and you won't book a project meeting at the same time as the school concert.

Plan transition time

Transition time is the gap between one activity and the next. If your diary is full of back-to-back meetings, you don't have any transition time. That can be a huge source of stress. Be realistic about the amount of time you need to physically or mentally move between meetings. For example, make sure the meetings you are in control of are not scheduled back-to-back. You can schedule your meetings for 45 minutes, and that gives you a 15-minute window if you have another meeting starting at the top of the next hour. Use that time to mentally prepare or take a bathroom break, for example.

One of my biggest stressors in the office was back-to-back meetings. I would spend time the day before or early in the morning making sure I had all the papers ready for the meetings, and a printed-out calendar of where I was supposed to be when. I'd make empty documents for meeting minutes so I could save time getting the notes out from each conversation.

And then I had children.

I constantly managed their transitions between activities, like giving countdowns: 'We can play for ten – five – three – one more minute and then we are going home.' But my own transitions went more like: *It's 5.25pm and I have to leave the office in five minutes. I can totally fit in writing another email before I go.*

When I realized, I started winding down from work 30 minutes before I needed to walk out the door. Now I check my To Do list and make sure the big things are done (and finish those straggler tasks like sending that half-written email I started at 8am). I mark the most important things for tomorrow so I know what to focus on. I do end-of-day things like change my out-of-office message, take my cups back to the kitchen, a last-minute check-in with my team. It's a calmer end to the day.

Book weekly reviews with yourself

Book a 15-minute review with yourself every week. It can happen at any time in the week, but make it a regular slot. Use the time to review your calendar for what's coming up. Look through your project portfolio list and remind yourself of what is outstanding – not for the project team but for you personally.

It is very easy to fall behind on projects when you are managing multiple things (and very difficult to catch up again), so a quick scan through your list of projects will help refresh your memory on what's a priority and what you could do to keep each project moving forward. Reflect on which projects are getting most of your time and adjust that for the coming week if necessary.

Track your time

Time-tracking software is worth using if you have access to it and are in an organization that has a culture of time management and time tracking. If you don't have access to that, just keep a note of what you are doing for a couple of weeks and you'll soon get a feel for which projects are taking up most of your time. Look back through your calendar to see how many meetings you had about each different project.

Your time tracking does not have to be accurate, or even something you do every week. The goal is simply to be aware, and conscious of which projects are sucking up all of your time. Conversely, the time-tracking information should help you identify which projects are not moving on, because you're not in a position to give them the time that they need.

If you identify projects that are not making progress due to how you are spending your time, look at your priorities and see what can be moved around to make more time for the lagging project. That might involve talking to your manager or project sponsor about how realistic it is to continue moving ahead with everything right now. Use your project portfolio list to help frame your workload.

Know your high-energy times

It is unrealistic to feel you can keep the same pace of work throughout a full day. Think about when you feel most energized. Perhaps it's the morning, when you are coming to your work fresh from a brilliant night's sleep. Perhaps it's the evening, as you're a night owl. Try to schedule your difficult, most thought-inducing work at the times when you have most energy. At its most simple, that means not scheduling strategic meetings for just after lunch when many people have a bit of a post-lunch slump.

Your personal energy levels and enthusiasm for work change throughout the week, month and year. Women may find their energy levels and ability to concentrate fluctuate with the hormone changes that come from the menstrual cycle.

It is not possible to perfectly plan your time around your preferences and moods – managers are unlikely to be receptive to the idea that you only do creative work on certain days, for example. However, where it is within your control to make choices about when to do work, use that to your advantage.

If working during your high-energy times doesn't resonate with you, try 'eating the frog' instead. The term comes from Brian Tracy's popular book, *Eat That Frog!* (2017) and refers to the saying that if the first thing you do each morning is to eat a live frog, the day only gets better from there. Tracy says that your 'frog' is the biggest, most important task that will give you the most positive impact today, and also happens to be the one you are most likely to procrastinate on. Do your hardest task in the morning and you can go about the rest of the day with a sense of accomplishment.

Deal with the guilt

Let's say you want to spend a couple of hours drafting out the plans for two projects and considering how they integrate so you can manage them together. You have blocked time in your diary for that, and perhaps even booked a meeting room to work in so you aren't physically at your desk where you could be easily interrupted. If your office culture is one where everyone seems to want everything done instantly, you may feel nervous about being 'away', even for two hours. This is something I hear frequently from the people I mentor: they don't want to be perceived as unavailable in case something important comes up.

It is time to set boundaries. Be realistic: what is it that could possibly happen within a two-hour window that would need your immediate attention? Perhaps a critical component failure, some kind of system outage or breakage, or a high-profile customer complaint or news story that needs a timely response – there could be situations where you need to be reached. That's OK. You have a 'drop everything list' (see Chapter 5) to help streamline incoming enquiries. Tell your colleagues what you are doing and that you'd prefer not to be disturbed unless it's urgent.

More often than not, you'll be able to spend a couple of hours on focused work and no one will even realise you didn't check your messages during that time. Try it!

A study from Columbia Business School (Bellezza et al, 2017) showed that high social status is conferred on people who are seen to be busy. They are perceived as competent and ambitious. Be deeply honest with yourself: do you think there is a sliver of a chance that some of your busyness is caused by *wanting* to be seen to be busy? Do people in your organization value busyness? The study also found that people wearing a bluetooth headset were perceived as competent, ambitious and of high social status. Perhaps investing in a headset to wear (even if you never took calls on it) would balance the need to be seen as constantly busy.

Let people know where you are

Set expectations with your colleagues by making the most of out of office messages and system alerts. This is especially important if you are going to be out of the office for any length of time. In *The Burnout Epidemic*, Jennifer Moss (2021) recommends adding a one-day buffer to your out of office message: tell people you are back at work the day after you actually come back. Your immediate team will know that you are back, but colleagues in your extended network might hold off chasing you for another day. That should buy you some time to catch up at your own pace.

Change the presence setting in your collaboration tools to 'away'. Put a message on your voicemail and email saying that you are unavailable at the moment, or not able to read emails until after lunch, or whatever. When people know you are working on something, they are more likely to try to contact you once and then leave you alone as they know their message has reached you and you will get to it when you can. If you are concerned about being unavailable, use the message to let people know how they can reach you in an emergency.

Another thing to try is having open door times. If your team is constantly interrupting, allocate some time where they know it's OK to do that. During the open-door time, they can come to you with anything and you will stop and work with them on whatever problem, question or challenge they are bringing to you. If they need you at another time, they know to wait until your next open-door slot, or scheduled meeting. This won't work in every situation but for some organizations it might be a way of managing constant interruptions if you feel that your team is constantly leaning on you.

Avoid decision fatigue

Project work involves a lot of decisions. By the end of the day, your brain can feel overwhelmed with the effort of having to make choices – and not just those related to your work. On average, people make 226 decisions just related to food per day (Jarrett, 2007), so imagine how many work-related decisions and other decisions your brain is processing every day. Knowing that decision fatigue is a possibility gives you the power to influence your environment and the way you approach your work to try to avoid it, or at least to minimize the impact. Template everything you can. Never start a document from scratch if you can help it. Someone else in the team probably has a similar document they've made in the past, or the Project Management Office might have a template you can use. Once you've written a document, like a project charter, always call up your last project charter and use that as the basis from which to write your new project charter.

Using templates can help you get to tasks more quickly because there's a lower barrier to getting started. Feeling disorganized can stem from having 'leftover' tasks that should have been done but haven't yet. Meeting minutes are a good example. Try to send out minutes, using a standard template to speed up writing them, within

24 hours of the meeting taking place. Your memory of the discussion will be fresher, so overall the task will take less time than if you left it to next week. The quicker you can share the output from the meeting, the quicker the task is off your To Do list.

As well as project documents, you can create template responses for things you are asked a lot, or for emails you send regularly. Then simply copy and paste the text into your response, or create a macro or shortcut to do it for you.

Checklists are a kind of template for a repeatable process. Whether you have a Standard Operating Procedure, protocol, work instructions or a simple tick box list, guidance on what to do when takes away some of the mental load required to do the tasks and minimizes the need for you to make decisions. Checklists should also result in fewer mistakes and less rework. If you can systemize more of what you do, you can get through more things. There are some example checklists for project managers in Appendix 1.

If you want to take this idea even further, take a leaf out of the books of leaders like Mark Zuckerberg, Steve Jobs and Barack Obama, and curate your wardrobe in a minimalist way to reduce the decision about what to wear every day (Saul, 2016).

Avoid gold plating

Gold plating is a project management term that means adding in more features or doing additional work even though it is not necessary. The customer hasn't asked for additional work, and you may have reached a point of diminishing returns: there's no value in adding extra.

Project managers tend to be conscientious, detail-orientated people who want to do a good job, and that's a positive. But that tendency to want to deliver excellent results can sometimes tip over into a desire to make something the best it can possibly be, even if no one else cares at that point. You probably won't get an acknowledgement of your additional work that is commensurate with the additional effort you put in, and the task will take longer and potentially cost more. When you have multiple projects to juggle, it's important to recognize when work is good enough. When it's good enough, ship it! Consider it finished and move on.

Use fake deadlines

One thing that works for me is setting myself a fake deadline which is something you can try too. I say to myself: *I'll complete this business case review by midday. And I will get it done.*

That frees me up mentally to complete the work within a reasonable time period to give it my full attention for that time, and then it's done. Give yourself a time limit and you may find you can achieve more because you are focused within that window.

Learn to use your tech

According to research by the European Commission (2020) only 61 per cent of the EU population have basic software skills, and only 33 per cent have above basic digital skills. Given how much project management work relies on using software and being able to competently navigate the digital world, not knowing how to use your tech can be a major productivity saboteur.

> Even if you are a digital native, your colleagues and suppliers may not be. On one of my projects, we factored basic computer skills training into the change management plan for those who needed it, to increase the level of digital literacy in the user population before we launched a new software product that would change the way people did their tasks.

Technology will help you be more productive, but only if you can use it efficiently. Here are some suggestions for making the most of the digital tools you have.

- Get the fastest internet service you can, especially if you work from home. So much of what we do relies on the internet so don't waste precious time waiting for screens to load – plus, it's really frustrating!

- Improve your touch typing: the faster you can type, the faster you can get things done. If you don't touch type, learn! Failing that, get voice recognition software and dictate instead.

- Speed up your mouse: change your computer settings to increase your mouse speed, increasing it to double the original setting.

- Learn keyboard shortcuts: it's faster to use keyboard shortcuts than navigate menus, switch tabs or execute commands with a mouse. Print out a list of keyboard shortcuts for your most commonly used applications and practise using them.

- Turn off notifications: this is a common piece of time management advice, but have you actually done it? Mute notifications for your collaboration tools and emails to minimize digital interruptions.

- Use text macros or a text expander: set up your devices or apps so that when you type a certain short phrase, it is automatically replaced with the full text. This can save you time typing out standard text you use regularly, such as the company's name address, project details or even your name.

- Use images and audio: learn how to take and annotate screenshots and make short videos to better communicate with your team. Leave voice messages via apps instead of defaulting to text chat where you have that option.

- Use a password keeper: resetting your password every week because you can't remember it is a real time waster. Use a password keeper service to keep your passwords secure, as long as the tool is sanctioned by your corporate IT department.

Quick questions for prioritization decisions

Sometimes you need to make a quick decision on whether something is worth doing right now, or whether the smarter choice would be to put it off until later. Here are some quick questions to ask yourself in the moment to help you prioritize.

- Does it get you closer to a project deliverable? If so, perhaps that's worth making time for.

- Has someone important asked you for it? It's not always worth listening to the HiPPO (Highest Paid Person's Opinion – see https://exp-platform.com/hippo/ (archived at https://perma.cc/SRQ3-FNZ9) for an explanation of how the term HiPPO came about) but sometimes you can't avoid prioritizing work from senior managers.

- Is it to do with somebody else's lack of planning? Is someone else struggling because they have created a crisis by not acting on something early enough? What would happen if you let them fail? Consider the consequences of saying no to this task right now and what would happen if you didn't step up to help them out. Sometimes the right thing to do would be to let them sort out their own mess. If you do choose to do the work, or have to do the work, think about how you could avoid that happening again.

I was asked to write a report on something I didn't know much about the day before it was due to be submitted for an internal committee meeting. I wasn't able to say no as the person who asked was far more senior than me. I felt frustrated because I'm sure they had known the report was due. The committee met quarterly and creating the report was an action out of the last meeting. In other words, I could have had three months to write the report instead of eight hours. To avoid this happening again, I put the dates of future meetings on my calendar with a note to ask for a copy of the minutes. Then I could have a proactive conversation with that leader and get early warning of any tasks coming my way, so I could better manage my time.

Three techniques to improve focus

When you do get dedicated working time for moving your projects forward, it's good to have a couple of strategies to make the most of that time. There are three techniques to try described here: Sticky three; Time blocking; and Focus on the 20 per cent. If you have used them in the past, reflect on what made you stop using them. How could you adapt a technique to make it better suit your working style? If you haven't tried a technique, give it a go. You won't need to use all these techniques every day for everything. But having them in your toolbox means you can reach for them when the time is right.

Sticky three

The simplest technique is what I call the 'sticky three'.

At the end of the day, write your top three tasks for tomorrow on a sticky note and leave it somewhere you will see it in the morning. For example, stick it on your computer monitor, laptop or keyboard. The tasks on the sticky note should represent what you'd be happy to get done if you only had the time and energy to achieve three things. Those activities should form the backbone of your day.

When you arrive at work the next day, you are instantly reminded of the top three tasks that are your priority for the next eight hours. It's a really simple way of getting quickly focused and zooming into work mode, so you can make a start on the things that are going to add the most value to your day.

If you want to take it further, consider which of the tasks would be the priority if you could only find the time to complete one. How would you slim down your To Do list to really focus on prioritizing the project or task that is the most important today?

Time blocking

Time blocking, also known as batching, is where you group similar tasks together to avoid task switching. For example, spend time responding to emails: it doesn't matter what project they relate to, but you only work on emails for a fixed time.

Task switching is the term to describe moving between tasks. For example, you spend ten minutes on the phone, then switch to updating your plan, then make another call, then spend ten minutes responding to emails, and so on. This is ineffective: many studies have replicated the results of Rogers and Monsell's research in 1995, which showed that people were slower switching between tasks than carrying out the same task on repeat.

Activities that can be batched include:

- Filing and document management;
- Dealing with emails;
- Returning or making phone calls;
- Project reporting;
- Team one-to-one meetings (I used to schedule all my one-to-one meetings on a single day each month);
- People management tasks, for example noting holiday requests and scheduled absence on project schedules, contributing to staff appraisals by providing feedback to line managers;
- Creating similar types of assets, like project newsletters or presentations;
- Showing gratitude and celebrating success, such as making the time to thank people for their contributions on each project.

Using blocks of time for the same kind of activity reduces the mental load of task switching and allows you to both get more done and feel less overwhelmed with the work.

> Try to arrange as many meetings as you can on the same day with the goal of having at least one day a week without any meetings at all.

Focus on the 20 per cent

Vilfredo Pareto was a 19th-century Italian economist who demonstrated that 80 per cent of the land in Italy at the time was owned by 20 per cent of the population. This 80/20 rule has become a popular management maxim: the Pareto principle says that 80 per cent of your results come from 20 per cent of the inputs. In other words, there are probably only a few tasks you are doing that drive the majority of your project outcomes.

Prioritize your time by spending more effort on the 20 per cent of activities that get you the bulk of your results. Here's a quick exercise to help you identify what those are.

1 On one side of a piece of paper, write down the tasks you do regularly across your projects.

2 On the other side, write down some recent wins, successes or outcomes you are proud of.

3 Draw lines to link the tasks to the successes. Which tasks contributed the most to your achievements? Those are the activities that are making the most difference to you: your 20 per cent. Make sure you spend enough time on those tasks as they are influencing your outcomes disproportionately to other activities.

FIGURE 6.4   Focus on tasks that drive results

You will end up with something that looks like Figure 6.4. It should be relatively easy to identify the tasks that are having the most impact on your results. As results, successes, achievements and so on are what project managers tend to be judged on, it's useful to know what drives those outcomes. Do more of that because you know it works. However, bear in mind that sometimes 'what works' changes over time and as you involve other stakeholders in the work, so this is an exercise worth revisiting a couple of times a year to check you are still focusing on activities that really make a difference.

Improving your level of focus during the time you have to do your work will help you feel more on top of multiple projects. Hopefully, you will find yourself completing work faster but that shouldn't equate to taking more on. You were probably putting in extra hours anyway. The goal of this book is to give you the tools to get your projects done and leave the office on time so if you can structure your workload and achieve greater levels of productivity, think carefully about what you do with those extra hours.

Beyond productivity box ticking

You've read this far through the chapter and have a good idea about how to make the most of your time to maximize your productivity at work. The tools and techniques in this book work effectively for people who have a reasonable workload. If you implement them, you should find yourself with a more structured workload and the ability to keep your projects moving forward in a lower-stress way than before.

But what if you implement everything and still find there is too much to do? No time management techniques in the world will help you leave the office on time if you routinely have more to do than any human could naturally cope with. Talk to your manager about your workload – while the conversation might be awkward, it is your only choice. Be prepared with details about what you have done to improve your personal productivity and manage your projects effectively so you can evidence the changes you made and how they have not been enough. Don't struggle on because that leads to burnout. You are not a resource; you are a human who deserves a supportive work environment. If you don't feel that you can achieve that in this role, it could be time to look for somewhere else to work. Before you start scouring the internet for new jobs, read Chapter 7 and see if influencing your environment would help your situation.

It might also help to reframe what it means to be productive. A different way to look at productivity is not to focus on how many tasks you tick off in a day but on your results and your impact. Use what Elizabeth Grace Saunders, in her 2021 HBR essay, calls a 'values-driven schedule' to identify your personal priorities and be intentional with your time. She talks about curating your calendar to fit your priorities, whether those priorities are work engagements, exercise, family commitments or something else. In 50 years will it matter if you stay late tonight at work or say no to that meeting? Or would you prefer to look back on a lifetime of health, family relationships and a fulfilling personal life? What does productivity really mean to you?

In today's digital and project economy, productivity can be hard to define and measure objectively, especially for creative and knowledge workers. Measures of output that served the economy so well in the industrial revolution are less relevant to the workplace today, as the boundaries between 'work' and 'life' become more blurred for many people.

Research is now considering more holistic ways of capturing how knowledge workers are doing at work, by blending classic approaches to productivity with measures of well-being. Guillou et al (2020) use the term Time Well Spent to describe a rounded approach to evaluating time at work. They allowed research participants to define what Time Well Spent meant to them over a working week and then analysed the results. They concluded that Time Well Spent is a blend of:

- What you work on: the researchers found that study participants valued making progress, following their plans and delivering a quality output.

- How you work: meeting deadlines, being focused and being efficient were self-identified measures of Time Well Spent.

- How you feel: the researchers found that a sense of satisfaction and achievement, as well as being involved in meaningful work and having fun contributed to personal definitions of Time Well Spent.

- How you take care of yourself: participants identified that Time Well Spent included paying attention to physical health (like eating well at lunch time), creating social bonds and looking after mental health and taking breaks.

If you get to the end of the day and haven't made as much progress on your projects as you would like, try to think holistically about how well your time was spent. There is as much value in training a new colleague or supporting a friend through a difficult time as there is in crossing something off your To Do list.

KEY TAKEAWAYS

- Be aware of the top three productivity saboteurs that affect your ability to move your work forward efficiently: procrastination, disorganization and poor planning.

- Personal time management is a blend of managing the flow of tasks coming in and responding to tasks in the most appropriate way. Constantly question whether the work has to be done or whether someone else is better placed to do it instead of you.

- Try out plenty of time management tactics so you have a grab bag of solutions available to use. Pick a few favourites and get into the habit of using them.

ACTION STEPS

Your action steps from this chapter are:

- If you suffer from any of the productivity saboteurs, block out 30 minutes in your calendar to brainstorm ways to approach your work differently.

- Review your task list and use the TIS task profiles to see the shape of your work. Which profile do you use most of the time? Is that the best use of your time? If not, what could you do to shift tasks around?

- Choose a few of the time management tactics and techniques in this chapter that are new to you and try them out.

- Productivity means more than what tasks got crossed off today. Consider what Time Well Spent means to you and how you judge and value your own time.

References

Allcott, G and Watts, H (2021) *How to Fix Meetings*, Icon Books, London

Allen, D (2002) *Getting Things Done: The art of stress-free productivity*, Penguin, Harmondsworth

Bellezza, S, Paharia, N and Keinan, A (2017) Conspicuous consumption of time: When busyness and lack of leisure time become a status symbol, *Journal of Consumer Research*, 44 (1), 118–38 (June)

Canfield, J, Hansen M V and Hewitt, L (2000) *The Power of Focus*, Health Communications Inc, Deerfield Beach

Csikszentmihalyi, M (2002) *Flow: The psychology of happiness*, Random House, London

European Commission (2020) Digital economy and society index 2020: Human capital. Available from digital-strategy.ec.europa.eu/en/policies/desi-human-capital (archived at https://perma.cc/Y2EQ-J9TR)

Guillou, H, Chow, K, Fritz, T and McGrenere, J (2020) Is your time well spent? Reflecting on knowledge work more holistically, *CHI 2020 Paper*, April 25–30, 2020, Honolulu. Available from www.merlin.uzh.ch/contributionDocument/download/12862 (archived at https://perma.cc/YD7A-YJXN)

Harrin, E (2021) Managing multiple projects: the research, 29 October. Available from https://rebelsguidetopm.com/managing-multiple-projects-the-research/ (archived at https://perma.cc/73XE-MV4Z)

Jarrett, C (2007) Mindless eating: The food decisions we don't realize we're making. Available from https://digest.bps.org.uk/2007/01/22/mindless-eating-the-food-decisions-we-dont-realise-were-making/

Mark, G, Gudith, D and Klocke, U (2008) *The Cost of Interrupted Work: More speed and stress*, Conference on Human Factors in Computing Systems – Proceedings, 107–110. Available from doi.org/10.1145/1357054.1357072 (archived at https://perma.cc/437E-UVE3)

Moss, J (2021) *The Burnout Epidemic: The rise of chronic stress and how we can fix it*, Harvard Business Review Press, Boston

Rogers, R D and Monsell, S (1995) Costs of a predictable switch between simple cognitive tasks, *Journal of Experimental Psychology: General*, 124 (2), 207–31

Saul, H (2016) Why Mark Zuckerberg wears the same clothes to work every day. Available from www.independent.co.uk/news/people/why-mark-zuckerberg-wears-same-clothes-work-everyday-a6834161.html (archived at https://perma.cc/4NUG-L2CU)

Saunders, E G (2021) 'Does your schedule reflect your values?' In *Getting It All Done*, Harvard Business Review Press, Boston

Schultz, E and Schultz, M (2021) *Not Today: The 9 habits of extreme productivity*, BenBella Books, Dallas

Tracy, B (2017) *Eat That Frog!* 3rd edn, Berrett-Koehler Publishers Inc, Oakland

Udemy (2018) *2018 Workplace Distraction Report*. Available from research. udemy.com/wp-content/uploads/2018/03/Workplace-Distraction-Report-2018-2021-Rebrand-v3-gs.pdf (archived at https://perma.cc/Y7HV-ZSJN)

Further reading

Adachi, K (2020) *The Lazy Genius Way*, WaterBrook, Colorado Springs

Cox, C (2021) *The Deadline Effect*, Avid Reader Press, New York

Thomas, M (2021) *From To-Do to Done*, Sourcebooks, Naperville

07

Concept #5: Positioning: setting up the environment for success

The final concept in the framework is positioning yourself and your environment for success, as shown in Figure 7.1. This means critically evaluating the processes and working practices you and your team have adopted by default and establishing if these could be tweaked to give you back some time. That goes for project documentation too: by the end of this chapter you will be equipped to decide what files you really need to create in order to lead, manage and control the work.

FIGURE 7.1   The Positioning concept in the managing multiple projects framework

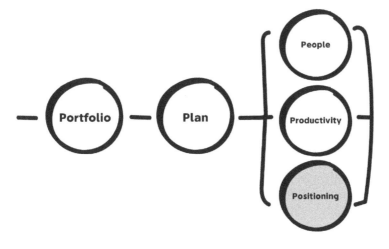

Your physical environment also shapes how you approach your work. In a 2020 study by iQ Offices, 73 per cent of respondents said they estimated they could save up to two hours a day if they worked in an office that was designed to minimize distraction. The impact of the physical environment was rated a greater productivity challenge than things like getting too much email. Offices that are too noisy, that don't offer private spaces and have poor natural light were all cited as reasons that negatively impact productivity.

While you can't always influence your office environment, you can control your home working set up. Microsoft's *Work Trend Index* (2021) reports an interesting challenge: 73 per cent of employees want the option for homeworking but 67 per cent report wanting more face-to-face time with their teams. That points to the trend for hybrid working; splitting time between the office and home. This chapter provides some tips for ensuring you have a home working set-up that supports your ability to work successfully.

Also in this chapter, you will learn how to develop a time maximizer mindset to free up more time for your future self. You'll get a step-by-step approach for standardizing things you do regularly to minimize decision fatigue and leave your cognitive capacity for activities that really do need thinking power. You will uncover how to combine risk management and governance processes, so they are more powerful and less time consuming.

The time maximizer mindset

There is a lot in your project environment that you cannot control, but you can adopt a time maximizer mindset. This is where you focus on what you can do today to make things better, faster or easier tomorrow. For example:

- Creating a process so you can repeat the work easily next time (more on that in the next section).
- Training a colleague so they can pick up the work from you.
- Creating a template.

- Setting up an automation, workflow or macro to do the work for you.

- Learning formulas or shortcuts to speed up how you do the work.

- Renaming files to make them easier to find in the future before saving them.

- Consolidating action logs or To Do lists into one master list or tool.

- Transferring sticky notes into a task management app.

- Booking a set of meetings in one go instead of individually.

- Reflecting on what works and what doesn't work so you can take active steps to do more of what works in the future.

The time maximizer mindset is about making sure the work you are doing today is setting you up for future success – or at least not undermining your success by making things harder for your future self. It requires an investment of time today with the knowledge that will pay off in the future, and that's what is hard: carving out the time in the short term to create an environment for longer term productivity and success. The more you consciously reflect on whether you are maximizing your time for the long term, the easier you will find it.

The five-email rule

In *Beyond Collaboration Overload*, Rob Cross (2021) talks about 'channel inefficiency': the misuse of meetings, email, text messages and so on. Failing to use those channels in the best way contributes to a culture of poor collaboration, which is an inefficient use of time. One time maximizer to make better use of your communication channels is the five-email rule.

This rule transformed the way I dealt with my inbox. When an email chain gets to five messages, it needs to stop being an email. If it isn't resolved within five messages, the subject must be so complicated, or there are so many additional points that need to be considered, that the team needs to move it to another collaboration channel, such as having a call or meeting about it. We started shifting to having those meetings at the point that we hit five emails, because it was clear that there were too many voices to be heard or too much information to be discussed effectively on a long email trail.

Changes in behaviour, like the five-email rule, can be introduced as new norms for your team. It takes time to position your environment for success, but soon you will be spotting opportunities to maximize your time – and that of other people – in many places.

How to standardize your work

Another common time maximizer that it is worth considering in more detail is standardizing processes you do often to reduce the mental overhead of having to think about the steps each time.

Decision fatigue, as we saw in Chapter 6, is when you have made so many decisions that you feel washed out at the idea of having to make any more choices. I noticed this explicitly after a long, difficult day at work when my husband asked me what I would like for dinner: I could not will myself to have an opinion. Decision fatigue is a type of mental exhaustion. When the choices relate to dinner, the consequences are not important, but when they relate to purchasing decisions, communication or training needs or risk mitigation activities, then they could affect how successful your project becomes.

When your brain is full of all the things to do on your projects, it feels like the amount of processing power available for how those things will get done is reduced. Standardizing the way things are done helps to limit the number of decisions required and stops you making poor choices. Many activities within project management are repetitive and lend themselves to a standardized process, checklist or work instructions that enable the team to work in a consistent and repeatable basis. If your Project Management Office already provides standard processes for these, then use your corporate guidance. However, if you are in an organization or role where standard approaches are not documented you will have to create your own process documents or checklists. The following four steps will show you how.

Step 1: Decide on the topic

First, decide what activity is the focus of your process. Find something you do that is repetitive (you don't have to do it every week) and that requires you to remember multiple steps or items. For example:

- Reviewing and managing risks and issues;
- Handling incoming change requests and deciding whether to take them forward or not;
- Preparing for a meeting and following up afterwards;
- Gathering data for monthly reports and then writing up the reports;
- The things you need to do prior to, during and after staff annual reviews for your team.

Step 2: Break the activity into tasks

Break down the activity into component tasks that represent each part of what needs to be done. If it is important that the steps are done in a particular order, you are creating a process. If it doesn't matter in which order the tasks are done, a checklist format will work well.

Step 3: Document the standardized approach

Choose how to document or format your list. There are apps for process creation, or you could create a simple spreadsheet, with space to tick off a task as complete, and print it out to use each time. Consider your working style and what would be the easiest for you to use.

Step 4: Test it!

Now you have created a process document or checklist, you should test it. That ensures you have remembered all the important points for this particular activity. The next time you need to complete this activity, pull out your process document or checklist and use it to work through all the tasks. You may want to add more steps or change the order. Your checklist can always be a work in progress – add things to it as you learn from the experience of using it.

It will probably feel basic and a little bit pointless to document things at this level, especially if you are not a junior member of the team. You may have been managing risks, issues and changes, organizing meetings and managing reporting for years. You can hold these processes in your head... can't you?

Yes, you can. But there is a lot of other stuff in there too. Having it written down takes away the thinking overhead when you are stressed and juggling a lot of work. And if you're managing multiple projects, you're probably stressed and juggling a lot of work frequently. Standardizing your processes means you are not starting from scratch every time. It alleviates some of the mental burden of having to use your active brainpower to think about these things, leaving you more capacity to focus on activities where you really do have to use your critical thinking faculties.

> Standardization is important. If working with a group of project managers that share project team resources, it is helpful if there is standard communication from all project managers, rather than one project manager sending reports and updates that are different in style and content from another project manager.
>
> Kelly, PMP, PMI-ACP, senior project manager, USA

The goal with standardizing processes is to make your work easier to repeat and simpler to manage. The more streamlined the approach, the more you will benefit from reducing the mental overhead of having to do things from scratch each time, even if it is an activity you are familiar with and do regularly.

Multi-project risk management

Another thing you can do to influence the environment for success is look at how you're managing project risk. Project risk management is the process of reflecting on what potential problems your project could hit and what you could do about them to make the impact or likelihood of occurrence less. Project teams regularly review their work to identify new risks and check that management actions for existing risks are on track.

However, there is another level to consider when you manage multiple projects: how all the open risks across all your projects combine to change the overall risk profile. Projects interrelate and often the big picture across all your projects looks quite different to the position on each individual project. A research study of 177 projects (Teller et al, 2014) concluded that the risk management process and the integration of risk information at portfolio level increases the positive effect on portfolio success. In other words, researchers have proven that it is worth consolidating risks across your projects because doing so increases the chance that all the projects will be more successful.

For example, let's say you identify a risk that a resource might not be available during August due to holidays. That might be a small risk for one project, one that's easily managed by shifting the work around in the team so your absent colleague catches up when they are back. But if that individual has tasks to complete on five of your projects, suddenly it's looking a lot less likely that they will be able to easily catch up on their return. Perhaps you need a different solution, like training someone else how to do the tasks so they can cover during holiday time.

Over 80 per cent of project managers do not consolidate risks across multiple projects to see if the combined effect of a risk is greater than individual effect, as you can see in Figure 7.2. That figure, drawn from a survey for this book (Harrin, 2021), is not surprising: project risk management is not currently taught in that way. Creating a consolidated risk profile is something typically done by the project management office to show the overall risk exposure for a portfolio across a department or division.

As a multi-project manager, you already take a portfolio view for managing your workload, and risk can be done in the same way. Carry out your risk management and planning activities twice: once

FIGURE 7.2   Per cent of project managers who have a multi-project approach to risk management

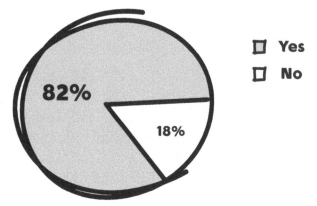

for the individual project and once at your personal portfolio level so you can see whether the impact of any risk changes when it is viewed in light of the risks from other projects. Look for connections or overlaps between the risks and see if that changes how you want to respond to them. Here are some common risks that become more impactful the more projects they apply to:

- Poor planning, new changes and unplanned work on one project may affect others.
- Poor project governance on one project may affect others.
- Changing priorities may affect other projects.
- Delays accessing shared resources, equipment or materials may affect other projects.
- Unavailable decision-makers may delay activity on more than one project.
- Projects may have dependencies to or from high-risk projects.

It's also worth considering adding risks that reflect the size of the project manager workload and the risk that too many projects are using the same resources, if these apply to your situation.

I manage strategic operational projects within the business and there are also departments that do very small projects, but in high volume. There are various tools in use across the business from simple products to power reporting tools. Some of them are intuitive; others have a good view at project level but don't provide a portfolio overview. I switch platforms from day-to-day depending on the project I'm contributing to at the time.

I would recommend looking for some sort of consultancy, if you have the budget, to get a company to configure a platform for you. They will go through a briefing process to understand what you are trying to do and what information you need. Many companies can take your existing solutions and help you use them more efficiently, tweaking what you have to make it do what you need.

Omar Warrack, supply chain project manager, UK

Multi-project governance

The role of governance on projects is to provide an ethical framework for decision-making and a set of standard good practices for managing the work. It ensures there is a system of checks and balances to make sure the right work is being done within appropriate, transparent, boundaries relevant to the methodologies in use.

Governance is unfortunately often seen as an overhead for organizations and project managers alike, but it is the collective conscious of the project, providing the direction and clarity of purpose for the team. Governance processes are often set up to support individual projects, for example project boards and steering groups convene to discuss a particular project or programme.

Therefore, it is worth looking at the governance processes for managing multiple projects to see if there are ways you can influence your environment to work better for you. Two key areas to consider are governance meetings and reports.

Governance meetings

Project boards or steering groups are made up of the key decision-making stakeholders that represent the customer, the supplier and anyone else who has a senior position and influence over the project. The smaller this group, the easier it is: chairing a steering group of 15 senior executives, each with their own opinion to share, is a tricky job! Typically, this meeting is chaired by the project sponsor, although the project manager normally does a lot of the preparation and talking in the meeting, guiding the group through the agenda and presenting any items that need action or decisions from this audience.

People managing multiple projects may have a small set of attendees at the project board meetings, or perhaps only meet with a project sponsor. As projects tend to be smaller (although not always), there are fewer stakeholders involved in the meetings.

Look at your workload overview and personal portfolio, and remind yourself of the groupings you created. The projects that fall into groups could be reviewed by the governance functions at the same time. For example, where you have three projects that fall under the same sponsor, hold a joint project board meeting where you discuss all three. That saves everyone present time and allows interdependencies between projects to be discussed more easily.

Reporting

Write joint reports where the projects have clear commonalities, or dependencies, and try to consolidate as much as you can into one document. This works if you have common metrics for tracking progress and performance, and can create a template that shows the information for every project.

Roadmaps are a good way to visually represent the progress of a selection of projects, for example all the projects you are working on for one department. Many software and graphic tools allow you to create a multi-project view of timelines or status, or you can draw a roadmap on your whiteboard or on flip chart paper during a workshop, then stick it up in the office where the team can see it. A roadmap showing multiple projects can help the team understand the priority and progress of projects in relation to each other.

Keep multi-project reports as simple as possible. There is a simple weekly project report template in Appendix 2, which is suitable for emailing to stakeholders; or take a look at the monthly table format template in Chapter 5. Stakeholders can always ask for more information and you can update your template for next time.

Agree governance parameters before you start

While you can merge governance meetings and project reporting, you do want to take stakeholder expectations into account. They may feel it is appropriate to have some projects taken together and discussed in one session, but others should not – for whatever reason – be covered in the same forum.

Talk to your project sponsor and agree the parameters for governance as soon as you can. Ask whether consolidating this project into other meetings or reports would be an approach they could support. Perhaps they are open to trying it and seeing how it works. Stay flexible and encourage your stakeholder community to consolidate and think holistically about the project portfolio, just like you do – although they may still expect certain meetings or reports to be focused on a single initiative. Stay flexible and update templates or meeting agendas as the project progresses. It's common, for example, to reduce the number of project board meetings if a project is going well and the project leadership team have confidence in the work. On one large project we moved from monthly project board meetings at the beginning to bi-monthly and then quarterly meetings as the project stabilized during the delivery phases.

My first experience with [managing multiple projects] was in a new job that did not have a well-defined project management structure. Business ownership of the projects was at bare minimum, so I had to do the heavy work of coaching all project stakeholders on the different roles they needed to own to successfully run the projects. I had extensive support from the leadership team, after several sessions of how projects should be structured for success. Eventually, after setting up a sort of framework, we were able to de-prioritize some projects and focused more keenly on those that were deemed must haves/ Urgent and Important. From this experience I learnt that when you are able to demonstrate value to people, they are more likely to join and support you in the journey. A clear goal and vision articulately defined and objectives drawn out is a good way to keep the team moving.

Akola, project/programme manager, Germany

Project documentation

Project documents are the files you create to manage, control and deliver the project. The documents you use are likely to reflect whether you are using an iterative, hybrid or predictive methodology.

There are lots of documents mentioned in the body of literature for project management knowledge and best practice. It seems like there are logs and files for everything. If you are building a massive Olympic park, or a military battleship, then there are higher standards for documentation, but for most projects done in office-based environments by small, medium and even large-ish firms, your time will be best spent on getting the basics right and avoiding creating documentation that does not add value to the way you want to manage the work. When you have to duplicate paperwork for each project you lead, you don't have time to create endless files that most stakeholders won't read. Instead, focus on the nine essential documents and adapt that list to suit your environment. They are:

1 Business case;

2 Charter;

3 Project management plan;

4 Schedule;

5 RAID log;

6 Status reports;

7 Budget tracker;

8 Lessons learned log;

9 Closure document.

1 Business case

At the concept or idea phase of a project, someone comes up with a bright idea. That is written down into a formal project proposal or business case. It's written to explain why the project should happen and it summarizes the problem the project is going to solve. It could be as simple as an email sent to the product owner outlining a suggestion for a new feature. It could be a fully costed business plan for the launch of a new product. Assuming the business case or proposal is taken forward, it is the driver that kicks off the whole project.

The business case is normally written by someone other than the project manager, usually the person who ultimately becomes the project sponsor. However, on small projects or those where you work closely with a department lead, it's possible you will get involved in the creation of the proposal in your capacity as project manager. In fact, I'd argue that it is preferable. It's certainly easier leading a project where you fully understand the background and context for why it was kicked off in the first place.

Whatever your business case or proposal looks like, there should be something that explains why this project is a good idea. Once the decision-makers have approved it, the idea can be formally ratified as a project.

2 Project charter

Before the project begins, the team should create the charter. It varies in format depending on the project approach you are using. The Agile Alliance recommends a single-page charter for agile projects. I prefer to use a fully rounded version that internally we call a Project Initiation Document. You might also hear the document referred to as a Project Brief.

Whatever you call it, the point of this document is to include everything you need to know about where the project is starting from, at least at high level.

Charters normally include a selection of these elements:

- Project objectives;
- High-level statement of scope;
- Key success criteria and critical success factors;
- High-level assumptions, constraints and risks known at this time;
- High-level project timeline;
- High-level budget;
- Expectations for resource requirements.

Often, much of this information can be extracted from the business case or proposal and expanded as necessary to provide greater detail for the project team.

> In my role, I often work on multiple projects across various stakeholders and teams. The most challenging hurdle to overcome is the lack of and miscommunication that occurs. One thing I'm trying to work on is creating more documentation for all projects (project briefs, complete timeline, the scope of work, etc.) to ensure stakeholders are on the same page. I've learned that communication is the most critical component of all projects within my organization and that it's easier to document the project along the way rather than have to reconnect with stakeholders down the road. I know that to do my best work when managing projects, I need all stakeholders to be on the same page and have a clear, accurate understanding of the project outcomes.
>
> Alyssa Towns, business operations specialist, USA

3 Project management plan

The project management plan in predictive methodologies has traditionally been a substantive document. It sets out how the project work will be done. At a high level, that's a statement of what approach will be used, for example the particular agile framework the team will adopt, or how work will be phased with a predictive approach.

A project management plan covers the expectations, method and approach for:

- Managing requirements and scope;
- Managing the schedule;
- Managing the budget and costs;
- Managing risks;
- Managing changes;
- Managing quality;
- Managing human resources and engaging stakeholders;
- Managing communications;
- Managing procurement and configuration if applicable.

These topics can be covered in individual documents or a consolidated document that covers all the topics, and this list is not exclusive. You might need a release plan that explains how releases will be managed, or a test plan outlining the team's approach to testing. Create what you need.

Organizations with a project management office tend to have structured approaches for doing these things anyway. There is probably a corporate or department risk management process that you can use for your project. It's not practical for every project manager to approach supplier management and procurement in a different way so there are probably internal processes for that too. Therefore, quite a few aspects of the project management plan might be covered by 'normal' ways of working within your organization.

Don't reinvent the wheel. There is little value in creating a document that repeats processes that exist elsewhere. You can simply mention in the charter that you will follow applicable internal processes as relevant. Perhaps your project needs agreement on how to secure resources, so it is appropriate to write down a plan for how that will happen, but you don't need a detailed plan for the other sections. Tailor and adapt so that you get the right level of document-ation for your project.

4 Project schedule

The project schedule sets out all the tasks, who is going to do them and when they are going to be done. It also tracks dependencies between tasks. Schedules can be created in a number of formats from a Gantt chart to a sprint plan, a timeline on a slide or a countdown plan in a table. Use whatever format works for you and your team, and meets the expectations of your stakeholders. Chapter 4 covers multi-project scheduling in detail.

5 Project RAID log

RAID stands for:

- Risks;
- Actions (and/or Assumptions);
- Issues;
- Dependencies (and/or Decisions).

I use the term 'RAID log' to cover all the different logs relating to the project. That includes all the elements in the list above, plus changes. RAAIDDC doesn't have the same ring to it!

The log could be a spreadsheet, software tool or something else that fits the team's working preferences. The objective is to have records of the daily activities and decisions to support project govern-ance and make sure everyone is on the same page. In a multi-project environment, you can have one log for each project or a consolidated system, depending on what works best for you and how you have grouped your projects into buckets.

6. Project status reports

Project status reports are another critical document. You are busy doing the work, so you need to tell people what work is going on.

They also help you track what's going on and provide information to decision-makers. They are the formal written record of progress.

There are lots of tools you can use to create real-time reports for individual projects. If your organization has mature software that can cope with displaying information at a programme or portfolio level, try to arrange your work so that you can take advantage of done-for-you dashboards. Macros, integrations, databases and using an API (Application Programming Interface) to connect different tools are other tech-enabled ways to create real-time reports.

Unfortunately, without software and a bit of investment, it's very difficult to create real-time reports and dashboards. The alternative is manually filling in a template on a regular basis: the trick is to make the template as simple as possible to complete, preferably using fields you can copy and paste from your project management software or records.

7 Project budget tracker

Your project budget is a different sort of document – it includes less text, and a lot more numbers. Many small projects that are largely focused on business change and process improvement will not have formal budgets at all, as the investment is usually in people's time. Alternatively, there may be a budget but it is wrapped up within a departmental budget which is managed by someone else and you need to work with them to purchase anything required.

If you are managing the finances for your projects, you probably want to keep the numbers separate. This is one occasion where there is limited benefit to combining data sets. Most managers will want granular reporting for money so budgets can be apportioned to the right client or cost code. Check with your sponsor before rolling up and consolidating budget information for your projects.

8 Lessons learned log

Reflection is an important part of the project management process. Throughout the project, ask yourself what is working and what is less successful. Ask your project team for their views too – there is a simple Stop, Start, Continue reflection exercise in Appendix 4. You may also be part of more formal reflection exercises like retrospectives or regular lessons learned discussions, either as the chair or a participant.

Lessons learned documents might not actually be documents. You could store your lessons learned in a database or wiki, or some other searchable format. Ideally, all the lessons should be made available to others in your organization so they are able to benefit from your learnings where appropriate. That helps mitigate the risk that information becomes 'lessons captured' instead of lessons truly learned and acted on.

9 Project closure document

Finally, when the project comes to an end you can produce a formal project closure document. In a formal environment, this document summarizes:

- What the project delivered;
- How the project performed against time, cost, quality and scope measures, i.e. were you late, over-budget or struggling to get a quality result?
- Any outstanding risks, issues and actions at the point of closure;
- The location of project files;
- Anything else the person receiving the handover needs to know.

In an informal environment, project closure could be achieved by sending an email or through the final set of minutes from team meetings.

Of all the documents, this is the most important one to get formally signed off and approved in some way. Without the project sponsor agreeing to the project being closed, the project is not closed. That means it stays on your personal portfolio and you'll be doing ad hoc work and support until they are happy that the work is delivered. That's a situation to avoid! You are busy enough with your portfolio and the goal should always be to close down projects smoothly, providing a handover to colleagues as necessary so you can move on to other things while leaving behind tidy archives of what happened in case people need to refer to the project history in the future.

The most important thing to remember about the documents mentioned above is that this section is only a guide to what project documents make the most difference when you are short of time and energy. Tailor the files you need so that you can best manage your project. Removing the admin time spent creating documents that don't add value means you can free up more time to lead your team. Overall, it's more important that the team members work together to deliver the project than they spend time creating paperwork that no one will ever read again.

> Working in the manufacturing industry, I have always managed multiple projects at the same time. The major difficulty seems to be getting a milestone completed before moving on to the next (new and shiny) project. It's easy to move on to something else, but not so easy to close out a project. Typically, this results from an outside force such as a component delay or a customer changing their mind with a design. The team then loses motivation to come back to it because they've already moved on to something that has a better chance of success, at least in the moment. Having consistent progress checks helps to keep the team on task, especially the act of reaching out to determine what each person specifically needs to take the next step. It's very difficult to manage schedules this way, so it feels like we're 'winging it' often.

> Sheri, senior project manager, USA

How to create a productive home office environment

Setting up your environment for success goes beyond having effective processes and ways of managing your work. It also stretches into making sure the physical environment where you work is a pleasant place to be, optimized for productivity.

The pandemic that began in 2020 and the shifts in the work environment that it created meant nearly 50 per cent of people did some work from home (ONS, 2020). Many organizations chose to maintain homeworking options for their teams, even after it was possible to return to the office environment. While there are many benefits to homeworking, not least avoiding the costs and stresses of the commute, there are also distractions at home that you don't have in the office. It's important to create a homeworking space that lends itself to your working style and what you want to accomplish while you are working from home. Small changes to your environment can give you a productivity boost and help you feel more in control of the work you have to do. Here are some considerations for achieving that.

Background noise

What kind of environment works for you? I prefer quiet when I'm working, but I live with people who prefer having music playing in the background. I have a dedicated workspace away from the house so I can have peace. You might find noise cancelling headphones or earplugs provide the same effect, or you might choose to have your music player close by so you can control the ambient noise easily.

Location

Where are you working? Some people feel more productive when they are connected to nature, and it's certainly possible to move your laptop onto a table in the garden or to an outside space if you prefer that. Many people feel more creative outside their normal work location – that's the reason we scheduled brainstorming workshops and training sessions in external meeting rooms.

Desk space

Do you prefer a standing desk? Or do you prefer sitting? There might be a way that you can configure your home office space to give you the choice to do both. Sometimes that can really help with lifting your energy and making you feel more productive. And it's also better healthwise to be moving around.

Whatever you choose, make sure your set-up is ergonomic and designed with your safety and comfort in mind. Choose a keyboard that is comfortable to use and follow the relevant health and safety guidance for display screen equipment usage.

Ambiance

Once you've found a space to work and got your desk set up, consider some of the other things that shape how you feel about your work zone. For example, bring some plants into your space. They increase oxygen levels, they look nice and they give you a sense of bringing in the outside: all proven productivity boosters.

Make sure the temperature is conducive to work. I find it very difficult to work when I am cold, and wear fingerless gloves in the winter. An air conditioning unit makes it possible to work comfortably when it's scorching hot. Control the temperature of your space so it doesn't distract you.

Make sure you've got enough light. This is really important if you are doing a lot of video calls, because it's easier to express yourself and to show your body language when your colleagues can see you. Make sure you have light preferably behind your camera so that the light comes on to your face during video calls.

Routine

Do you like to have a routine? Or do you prefer to be able to work flexibly? Some people prefer to have a very solid routine; others prefer to work flexitime around their other responsibilities, then make up the hours working early mornings or late evenings. As long as your manager and team are OK with your working schedule and routine, go with whatever works best for you.

Think about how you can use your routine and your time in the day to spend your energy when you have the most of it.

Distractions

Consider how you will manage distractions within your space. For example, can you hear the doorbell? If so, will you stop work to get up to open the door for deliveries? If you have children at home, ask them to make a sign for your work space for you to hang up when you cannot be disturbed. My office door has a lock so I can shut myself in during important calls. A physical ribbon or a rope across the door can also serve as a reminder to others at home that you are not in a position to be disturbed.

Make sure you have everything that you need in order to be able to work effectively, so you're not constantly having to get up and search the house for resources. You should have all your chargers in place so that you can use those. If you use things like external hard drives, make sure that you've got those and the relevant cables available as well. Buy duplicates if you can so that your kit doesn't have to ever leave the office space.

Having said that, you also need to build in breaks. In an office environment there are plenty of moments for screen breaks: walking to a meeting room, talking to a colleague; working at home, not so much. Never feel guilty about taking a break in your homeworking day. Take a walk, call a colleague or friend, or simply sit and have coffee outside or near an open window for a little bit of fresh air. Breaks can reset your brain and help you come back to work feeling more energized to get on with what needs to be done.

Working from home doesn't make you inherently more or less productive. You still need to be realistic about the amount of work you can get done in a day, so keep your To Do list manageable and limit the number of meetings you accept.

Influencing your office environment

If the considerations above help you at home, think about how you could make similar changes at work in the office. Could you agree guidelines on using headphones or earbuds for music as a team, along with how to interrupt or get the attention of someone wearing headphones? Is your desk set up as ergonomically as possible with adequate light for video calls? Do you have a way to regulate the temperature? What home comforts could transition to the office to make it a more comfortable work environment?

Start a conversation with your colleagues about what they enjoy about their home working environment and what they enjoy about the office and how to blend the best bits of both. In one office I worked in, a staff engagement survey highlighted the fact our team needed another coat stand, especially in winter. It was such a small (and cheap) fix for the management team and yet had a demonstrable impact on people's ability to transition smoothly into work in the morning. Changes don't have to be big to be meaningful.

Creating reflection time

Projects are dynamic environments. When you are dealing with the complexities of interrelated and overlapping strands of work, things change regularly. What used to work perhaps now doesn't have the same impact. Stakeholder expectations have changed, or maybe new stakeholders have joined the team and bring with them different working styles and communication preferences. That's why reflection time is important. It's a moment to take stock of what is working right now and how you can maximize and capitalize on the activities that are contributing to getting things done, helping achieve the results and making your life easier.

Looking for opportunities to continuously improve by learning as you go is the sixth and final personal portfolio management principle (for a recap, flip back to Chapter 3). It asks you to find time to consider what you have learned and what you are going to do differently as a result of that knowledge. Finding the time to reflect can be difficult when your project workload is heavy, but there are ways to build reflection time into each month. There are probably retrospectives or lessons learned conversations already scheduled: these are a rich source of learning and opportunity. Have a working lunch with a colleague in a similar role to you and chat about what you've done this month that was successful. Share ideas about how to approach the situations that didn't go quite so well. If you prefer to reflect alone, put 30 minutes in your calendar for first or last thing in the week, grab your favourite hot drink and work through the Stop, start, continue exercise in Appendix 4.

KEY TAKEAWAYS

- Your ability to make the most of your time and feel in control of your work is influenced by your environment.

- Cultivate a time maximizer mindset where you focus on what changes can be made that will set you up for success in the future.

- Standardize as much as you can to minimize decision fatigue and make it easier to work in a way that is repeatably good. Checklists, work instructions and processes can help.

- Consolidate project risks at portfolio level to assess whether the risk profile of your work changes when all projects are considered together.

- Combine governance frameworks across all your projects where it makes sense to do so.

- Create the right project documentation for your project so you have what is necessary for management and control without creating extra bureaucracy.

ACTION STEPS

It takes time to make changes to your environment, so pick something you want to improve on and make a plan to implement that. When that is done, choose something else. A slow and steady approach helps you avoid what Dorie Clark, in her 2021 book, *The Long Game*, calls strategic whiplash: a situation where you never see any results because you constantly change direction without giving your changes enough time to take effect.

Your action steps for this chapter are:

- Find one thing that you could take action on today (or in the next couple of days) to make it easier to manage your projects tomorrow.

- Introduce your team to the five-email rule and agree to try it.

- Identify where you have processes that could be documented. Pick one and turn it into a set of work instructions, a process document or checklist. Could you share the process with colleagues?

- Review the risk logs for each project together to create a consolidated view of risk across your personal portfolio. See whether the combined impact increases or decreases the risk.

- Consider how to consolidate the performance reporting and governance for your projects, if and where you can, and then put that into practice.

- Look at your home working environment if you have one and consider what you could improve to make it feel more like a workspace that is conducive to productivity.

References

Agile Alliance (undated) *Project Chartering*. Available from www.agilealliance.org/glossary/project-chartering/ (archived at https://perma.cc/QT7S-KA8U)

Clark, D (2021) *The Long Game: How to be a long-term thinker in a short-term world*, Harvard Business Review Press, Boston

Cross, R (2021) *Beyond Collaboration Overload*, Harvard Business Review Press, Boston

Harrin, E (2021) Managing multiple projects: the research, 29 October. Available from https://rebelsguidetopm.com/managing-multiple-projects-the-research/ (archived at https://perma.cc/73XE-MV4Z)

iQ Offices (2020) *57 percent of Canadians are distracted, lose up to 2 hours of productivity each workday*. Available from www.globenewswire.com/en/news-release/2020/02/10/1982254/0/en/iQ-Offices-survey-57-percent-of-Canadians-are-distracted-lose-up-to-2-hours-of-productivity-each-workday.html (archived at https://perma.cc/X4AB-L2R4)

Microsoft (2021) *Work Trend Index Annual Report: The next great disruption is hybrid work: are we ready?* Available from www.microsoft.com/en-us/worklab/work-trend-index/hybrid-work (archived at https://perma.cc/ZSZ4-SCPG)

ONS (2020) *Coronavirus and homeworking in the UK: April 2020.* Available from www.ons.gov.uk/employmentandlabourmarket/peopleinwork/employmentandemployeetypes/bulletins/coronavirusandhomeworkingintheuk/april2020 (archived at https://perma.cc/P5JW-J9FG) [Accessed 21 August 21]

Teller, J, Kock, A and Gemünden, H G (2014) Risk management in project portfolios is more than managing project risks: A contingency perspective on risk management, *Project Management Journal*, 45 (4), 67–80

Further reading

Vaden, R (2015) *Procrastinate on Purpose: 5 permissions to multiply your time*, Perigee, New York

Appendices

Final words

I want to end with this story from Kimberly, because the image of working in a fast-food environment but having customers who expect a sit-down service resonates so well with me, and I'm sure you will recognize it too.

> I work in a fast-food PM environment that expects sit-down service: I carry 12 clients and 32 projects across those clients. I'm one of nine, and I'm a programme manager. So I have mine, and then I have dotted authority to all the others for process and audits. I wish I had one single way of tracking what needs to be done, by when, and by whom. I have about 32 different ways because no one wants to be the same. It's hard. I have time set every day to work my lists, I alternate starting from the top alphabetically with starting from the bottom, but always attend to the loudest first. I have learned to give myself five minutes before each meeting to review my bullet items and reacquaint myself with the stakeholders and deliverables so that it seems, to them, that they and their projects are my only focus.
>
> Kimberly Ray, programme manager, US

Kimberly's story speaks to the reality of juggling multiple projects, the compromises we make and the hacks we use to try to make everyone feel as if their work is worthy of our full attention.

I hope this book has given you some tools and tips to manage the things you can manage. The goal was to provide you with practical ways to adapt your working style to help you feel like your time is well spent – and perhaps to make it more likely that you provide your colleagues with that sit-down service we all strive for.

The unfortunate reality is that the way many organizations manage work is broken. In my experience, too many leaders at all levels in the organization are unable or unwilling to say no to more work. There are personal and professional ramifications to having difficult conversations about workload and juggling multiple projects: *What if they think I'm simply not good/fast/efficient enough at doing my job? What if I truly am not good enough?*

It's hard to assess whether it is us or the job that is the issue. However, often the only part we can usefully influence is the way we approach the work. You can do the best you personally can in order to keep all the balls in the air but, at the end of the day, if your organization is not equipping you for success, that working culture can drain your motivation and eat away at your belief that your work is fulfilling.

Sadly, I find myself suggesting too often to talented, experienced project professionals that the time has come for them to move on from their current business and take their skills somewhere that is better set up to support productive working practices before they hit burnout. Once we have optimized their working practices and empowered them to have difficult conversations about processes, workload management, expectations and resourcing, there is often nowhere else to go except out.

The good news is that you are now equipped to have those difficult conversations. You can talk about how you have combined, streamlined and optimized your work so you can get more done in the time you have to serve your stakeholders more effectively. You've got tools to share and you can spread the word about what it takes to keep all your work moving forward. You're a grassroots campaigner for portfolio management: you do it at a personal level, and you can fly the flag for the organization taking it seriously as a broader, department, division or enterprise approach for getting work done. Ultimately, managing multiple projects shouldn't mean working more hours: instead, the onus is on us to come up with strategies to deliver what we need to and still leave the office on time.

The world of project management is expanding. More and more work is delivered as projects, and there is no sign that will change any time soon. You've got the skills to succeed in what

Antonio Nieto-Rodriguez in the Foreword calls the project economy and, if you choose, you can influence your organization for good.

But you don't have to do that right now. You're a busy leader; expect to take some time to reflect on what you've learned and implement the changes you choose. You're already doing enough, and I appreciate you carving out the time in your schedule to get to the end of the book.

Now breathe. And pop the kettle on. You've got this!

Appendix 1: Productivity checklists

These checklists are a starting point for thinking about daily, weekly, monthly and annual activities as a project manager. Use them as a prompt to ensure all of your projects are making progress and getting the attention they deserve, because it is easy to overlook the basics when work gets busy.

Daily things to do

- Review your To Do list;
- Check in with project team members who have tasks with upcoming deadlines or work that is stuck;
- Deal with urgent issues;
- Update the project schedule with changes;
- Update project action list with any progress;
- Deal with urgent emails, voicemails and messages;
- Review work for tomorrow and get ready for anything that needs preparing.

Weekly things to do

- Update the project schedule, reviewing actual progress against anticipated progress and take action accordingly.

- Review and act on project risks and changes.
- Check in with the team and have a status meeting if required.
- Check in with the project sponsor, product owner or senior customer as well as other key stakeholders and suppliers.
- Prepare and circulate a weekly report if appropriate.
- Review what's coming up next week and plan accordingly.
- Say thank you to the team.
- Plan for and prepare for upcoming project communications.

Monthly things to do

- Capture, review and act on lessons learned.
- Review milestones and key targets for next month and check they are on track to be achieved.
- Prepare and circulate monthly reporting.
- Review and update the project budget.
- Review resource allocation and make sure people are available for work due next month.
- Update project management documentation.
- Hold a governance review via a steering group, project board, client meeting or similar.
- Do some career development activity.
- Scan the horizon for potential issues and act accordingly.
- Review the business case and original proposal and ensure it is still viable.

Annual things to do

- Complete any year-end financial tasks such as accruals, budget carry overs and settling outstanding invoices.
- Input to or carry out staff performance reviews and schedule your own review with your manager.

- Input to the strategic plan, prioritization and resourcing requirements for next year if required.
- Organize a project celebration if you haven't had one recently.
- Check you've taken your annual leave and plan what to do if you still have time to take.
- Send greetings cards to vendors, colleagues and other stakeholders to mark the holidays.

Appendix 2:
Simple weekly project report template for multiple projects

The format below can be used to report progress on multiple projects within one document. You can use Red/Amber/Green colour coding to highlight text (where the recipient will receive the information in colour) to further draw attention to activities that are on track, at risk or falling behind. The template is designed to be used on a weekly basis but can easily be adapted to report once a month.

Subject: Weekly report for [project names/my projects/Marketing projects etc.]: [date]

Please find below the weekly report for the following projects for [date]:

- Project name 1;
- Project name 2;
- Project name 3.

Tasks due for completion this week:

Project name 1:

- Task 1 – outstanding;
- Task 2 – completed;
- Task 3 – meeting to discuss postponed until next week.

Project name 2:

- Task 1 – outstanding;
- Task 2 – completed;
- Task 3 – meeting to discuss postponed until next week.

Tasks for next week:

Project name 1:

- Priority task for next week 1;
- Priority task for next week 2 (Elizabeth);
- Priority task for next week 3 (meeting happening Tuesday).

Project name 2:

- Priority task for next week 1;
- Priority task for next week 2 (Elizabeth);
- Priority task for next week 3 (meeting happening Tuesday).

Other things of interest:

- Some news that doesn't fit into the categories above;
- An issue or new risk that everyone needs to know about;
- Some celebration of a good thing that happened;
- Upcoming holiday/vacation time/notice of future meeting dates.

Appendix 3: How to implement the framework

Reading this book is only the first step on your journey to becoming better at managing multiple projects. Next, you have to implement what you have learned. Below is a summary of the action steps in this book, plus some additional tasks that will help you implement the framework.

Remember, if you haven't been doing the action steps as you have been reading the book, that's OK. During your first read, you went through the book to familiarize yourself with the framework, the ideas and concepts. The checklist below will help you read it again with a view to taking action towards creating your own multi-project management system.

As a recap, there are five concepts within the framework: Portfolio, Plan, People, Productivity and Positioning. You can work through them one at a time, perhaps taking a concept per week (or month) to implement in your own work. If you know you will find implementing your new skills tricky, perhaps enlist the help of an accountability partner to work with you? You can review processes and talk together about the best ways to use the framework efficiently in your workplace.

APPENDIX TABLE 3.1   Framework concepts and action steps

Framework concept	Action step	✓
Pre-work	Identify what category your workload fits into. Do you have a sushi, spaghetti or side dish project workload? Or perhaps a blend of a categories?	
	Reflect on your current position. Do you spot any of the warning signs outlined in Chapter 2? If you are a team leader, can you spot the warning signs in anyone in your team?	
Portfolio	Create a workload spreadsheet (or equivalent) covering all the projects and major recurring tasks that you are working on.	
	Prioritize the work on your workload spreadsheet.	
	Look for connections between projects and group similar work into logical buckets.	
Plan	Make sure each of your individual projects has a schedule or timeline.	
	Map the dependencies between your projects.	
	Choose either the ladder or hot air balloon view to make your consolidated schedule (or decide to have a go at both and see which you prefer).	
	Combine your schedules into one overarching timeline.	
	Review that schedule to look for resource conflicts and busy times and take appropriate action.	
	Start an action log for task-level planning.	

TABLE APPENDIX 3.1   *continued*

Framework concept	Action step	✓
People	Identify all your stakeholders and create a stakeholder register and stakeholder map.	
	Review the power, legitimacy and expectation of urgency of your stakeholders across all of your projects, and use a table to identify stakeholder saliency and to help you prioritize where you spend your time.	
	Check everyone knows what is expected of them for each project and that they are only scheduled to work at 80% of their available hours.	
	Review your upcoming meetings and see what can be combined and which ones can be done in less time: change your default meeting time to at least ten minutes less than what it is now.	
	Look at your individual communications plans and see where it makes sense to consolidate and merge the information that is being shared with your stakeholders.	
Productivity	If you suffer from any of the productivity saboteurs, block out 30 minutes in your calendar to brainstorm ways to approach your work differently.	
	Review your task list and use the TIS task profiles to see the shape of your work. Which profile do you use most of the time? Is that the best use of your time? If not, what could you do to shift tasks around?	
	Choose a few of the time management tactics and techniques from Chapter 6 that are new to you and try them out.	
	Productivity means more than what tasks got crossed off today. Consider what Time Well Spent means to you and how you judge and value your own time.	
Positioning	Find one thing that you could take action on today (or in the next couple of days) to make it easier to manage your projects tomorrow.	
	Introduce your team to the five-email rule and agree to try it.	
	Identify where you have processes that could be documented. Pick one and turn it into a set of work instructions, a process document or checklist.	
	Review the risk logs for each project together to create a consolidated view of risk across your personal portfolio. See whether the combined impact increases or decreases the risk.	

TABLE APPENDIX 3.1   *continued*

Framework concept	Action step	✓
	Consider how to consolidate the performance reporting and governance for your projects, if and where you can, and then put that into practice.	
	Look at your home work environment if you have one and consider what you could improve to make it feel more like a workspace that is conducive to productivity.	
Finally	Reflect on what you have achieved and how it makes you feel about your workload. How can you share your successes with others at work?	

Appendix 4: Stop, start, continue

What's working for you right now? What's not? Take a moment to reflect on how the past month has gone and how next month can build on this (or be different).

Date: _____

STOP: What are you going to stop doing?

_____

_____

_____

START: What are you going to start doing?

_____

_____

_____

CONTINUE: What are you going to continue doing?

_____

_____

_____

More books by Elizabeth Harrin

Engaging Stakeholders on Projects: How to harness people power (APM, 2020)

Whether you work at a project, programme or portfolio level, you'll have stakeholders involved in your activities. This book addresses the challenges you face when dealing with project-drive change in organizations. It provides an in-depth examination of the topic covered in the *APM Body of Knowledge* (7th edition), providing projects professionals with detailed tips, tools and practical steps to help improve ways of working. It will show you how harnessing the power of people is key to improving project success.

This book addresses central questions such as:

- What does engagement look like?
- What tools have I got available?
- How do I best reach, engage and work with stakeholders?
- How do I minimize conflict and resistance to change and move toward resolution?

> Managing stakeholders is a critical skill required by all managers and finally there is a book to help you to do just that. As with every good book you'll want to read it front to back to begin with, however, there is so much practical content here that you'll be jumping around it in no time! It's suitable for every project professional regardless of sector, country or area of expertise. Even with 20 years of experience myself, I still was able to take plenty of things away!

> Colin D Ellis, author and founder of the Culture Makers community

Collaboration Tools for Project Managers (PMI, 2016)

Today's project leaders face the challenge of managing projects effectively using tested and reliable methods, while also trying out the new methods preferred by some global and tech-savvy team members and stakeholders. Information travels faster than ever before. Project teams are called upon to produce relevant and up-to-date project information, increase productivity and deliver results through top-notch communications.

Social media and online communications tools have rapidly changed our world outside the workplace. These platforms and other tools, like wikis and big data repositories, offer exciting possibilities to improve project team collaboration and stakeholder communication in the workplace as well. Since project managers rely on communication and effective team management skills, they need to keep up with the fast pace of change, technology trends and the latest business drivers that help move organisations forward.

This book builds on Elizabeth's 2010 book, *Social Media for Project Managers* and is fully updated. It provides the latest information, success stories and an easy-to-follow guide to implementing online collaboration tools successfully.

It's time for project teams to explore how online collaboration tools can help them to communicate faster, work virtually with people across the globe and get better business results.

> As project managers, we can no longer just manage our project details; schedule, budget, quality, scope. Yes, they do need to be managed, but it is becoming much more than that. One must, as Elizabeth says, 'Create collaborative environments where people can do their best work…'. That environment will not only make the project manager more effective, but will make the project more successful, something we all strive for. In her book, *Collaboration Tools for Project Managers*, Elizabeth does just that: help the project manager use all the collaborative tools available. She defines the tools, provides the reasoning behind their effectiveness, and how to use them for their maximum value. Elizabeth also provides a roadmap to a myriad of resources as well as inviting the reader into the conversation. This book is a must read for all project managers who want to be more effective, and I believe that is what we all want.
>
> David Shirley, PMP, author, educator and
> Cleland Project Management Literature Award Winner

Shortcuts to Success: Project Management in The Real World (BCS, 2013)

Anything from an office move to the Olympic Games can be termed a project but it takes time to gain the experience required to be confident on the job. Not any more: this book contains the wisdom of project managers totalling over 250 years of professional project management experience in a highly accessible format. This practical and entertaining book will help project managers get up to speed quickly with good practice, avoid pitfalls and deliver business value.

> Packed with hard-won insights on how to make projects work in today's pressurised business environment. Apply what it suggests and you're likely to save your company a fortune and yourself heaps of frustration!

> Dr Penny Pullan, PMP, director, Making Projects Work Ltd

Customer-Centric Project Management (Routledge, 2012). Co-authored with Phil Peplow

There has been a sea-change in the focus of organizations away from a traditional product or service centricity towards customer-centricity – and projects are just as much a part of that change. Projects must deliver value and the authors demonstrate convincingly that stakeholders are the ones who get to decide what 'value' actually means.

This short guide explains the importance of customer-centricity to project performance and demonstrates the tools and processes to guide customer-centric thinking in your project teams. The book provides a straightforward implementation guide to delivering engagement, even on difficult projects.

> [This approach] allowed us to achieve fantastic results in terms of customer satisfaction. It enabled us to channel our energies into precisely what our customers were looking for – a consistently excellent service.

> Neil Harrison, CEO, Travelex

INDEX

Note: Page numbers in *italic* indicate figures or tables

AUG – 8 2022

CPSIA information can be obtained
at www.ICGtesting.com
Printed in the USA
JSHW012250280422
25413JS00007B/62